"Calling is a long walk," says Lauren Brewer Bass. It's a "sacred journey. wc know more about that spiritual metaphor after metaphorically trailing her on the Camino de Santiago. Her pilgrimage of faith comes clearer because of her pilgrimage on foot. And so will yours along whatever way you travel with and to God.

—*George Mason*
Pastor, Wilshire Baptist Church
Dallas, Texas

Part Cheryl Strayed finding herself on the Pacific Crest Trail in *Wild,* and part Parker Palmer offering tools to seek the voice of vocation in *Let Your Life Speak,* Lauren Brewer Bass's *Five Hundred Miles: Reflections on Calling and Pilgrimage* takes the reader on a journey of God-shaped proportions as she listens honestly for the call of Love. Lauren beckons all who strain to hear that same call to join her on the winding path of pilgrimage, where the Spirit's companionship can both rub blisters and grant blessings. No matter the road you may be on, *Five Hundred Miles* will quickly become a trusted partner.

—*Emily Hull McGee*
Pastor, First Baptist Church
Winston-Salem, North Carolina

Lauren Brewer Bass's *Five Hundred Miles* is a sort of *Wild* for the Christian soul seeking to live its calling. Lauren tells the story of her experience of walking the Camino de Santiago in Spain as a way to imagine calling as a journey rather than a destination. Her insights will no doubt be an inspiration to young people who are setting out on their own paths to live their callings as faithful pilgrims.

—*Susan M. Shaw*
Professor of Women, Gender, and Sexuality Studies
Director of the School of Language, Culture, and Society
Oregon State University

This is the author's account of her pilgrimage along the Camino de Santiago in Spain. As her experience unfolds, it becomes a metaphor for traveling the path to discover one's calling in life. This book is much more than a recounting of a personal pilgrimage. It is an invitation and a blueprint for all persons of faith walking the path to authentic calling.

—*Joan Spero, SL*
Sister of Loretto

Smyth & Helwys Publishing, Inc.
6316 Peake Road
Macon, Georgia 31210-3960
1-800-747-3016

Library of Congress Cataloging-in-Publication Data

Bass, Lauren Brewer, 1986-
Five hundred miles : reflections on calling and pilgrimage / by Lauren Brewer Bass.
pages cm
ISBN 978-1-57312-812-4 (pbk. : alk. paper)
1. Christian pilgrims and pilgrimages--Spain--Santiago de Compostela.
2. Bass, Lauren Brewer, 1970---Travel--Spain--Santiago de Compostela. I. Title.
BX2321.S3B39 2015
263'.0424611--dc23

2015013839

FIVE HUNDRED

HUNDRED

miles

Reflections on Calling and Pilgrimage

Grace,

Blessings on you & your own
epic journey of calling!
(& much thanks for all your
kindness & support!)

Lauren Brewer Bass

Lauren

For David, my love,
and for all the other pilgrims
on this journey.

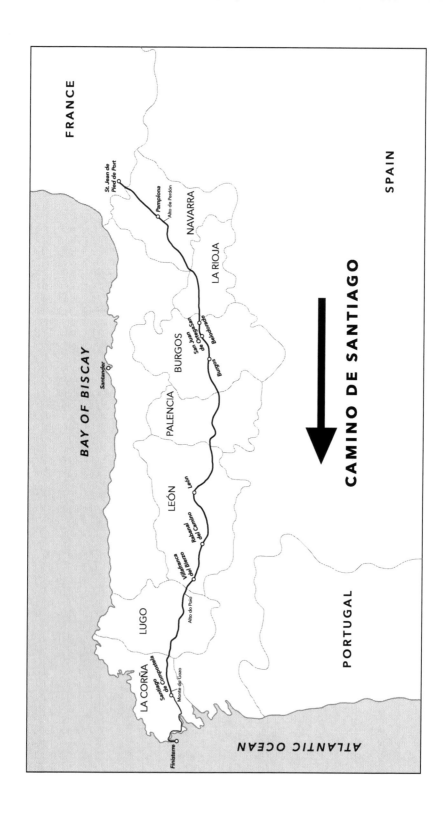

Contents

Foreword

by Pam Durso

Every book has back stories: fun stories about when or where the idea for the book emerged, stressful stories about writer's block and lack of inspiration, painful stories about computer malfunctions and printer jams, and unforgettable stories about seeing a book cover for the first time. With a world full of great books, there is also a world full of great back stories. But *this book*—this book has the best back story ever.

The story begins in 2011, two years after I became executive director of Baptist Women in Ministry. In my role to that point, I had spent much time encouraging and supporting the ministry callings of women seminarians. But in 2011, I realized that one area of need that was going unmet was the nurturing of college women who were in process of discerning a call to ministry. Luckily or perhaps providentially, Meredith Stone was serving at the time on the BWIM Leadership Team, and she agreed to help me plan and host a college-call retreat in Texas, where she then worked as Women in Ministry Specialist for the Baptist General Convention of Texas. We raised some money, planned a schedule, lined up leaders, and invited college women. As we were preparing for the retreat, Meredith wrote curriculum for us to use. As the time for the retreat drew near, we decided to invite a few seminarians and recent seminary graduates to round out our numbers.

On November 11, Meredith and I drove together to the Heart of Texas Baptist Encampment in Brownwood, Texas. We unloaded the car, set up the meeting room, and welcomed the participants. When we divided into small groups for discussion later that evening, sitting near me on a picnic table bench outside was Lauren Brewer, a recent graduate of Logsdon School of Theology. Over the course of the next twenty-four hours, I listened to the story of her calling, heard tales of her travels and adventures, and laughed and maybe cried a little with her and our newfound friends. The next day we said goodbye, but Lauren and I stayed in touch. We e-mailed some, talked on a phone a few times, and we became Facebook friends. That next year Lauren was in the midst of looking for a place of service, a ministry position, and she chose Denver (for reasons you will read in the following chapters). Her new work fascinated me, so I asked her to write posts for the BWIM blog about what she was doing in Denver. I soon discovered that Lauren is a gifted writer, a teller of beautiful stories, and a wise young woman.

Wait for it. I am getting to the best back story part here!

In fall 2013, I realized that BWIM needed a book. We needed a book about calling to share at future college retreats. We needed something creative and fresh. After all, our imaginations for ministry had evolved and expanded. Ministry was no longer one-size or even two-sizes-fit-all. Ministry in the twenty-first century encompasses wider and deeper opportunities for local church leadership that included pastoring, ministering with and among children and teenagers, guiding mission and outreach outlets, heading up community involvement, and equipping members in areas of spiritual formation and education. Ministry also encompasses chaplaincy in hospitals, prisons, and the military, leadership of non-profit organizations, building global networks, and so much more! Despite this greatly expanded vision of ministry, our conversations about calling and call discernment had not changed that much, and I realized that we needed an overhaul of our understanding as well as our language about ministry calling.

I called Meredith and told her that we needed a book. Her response was, "Call Lauren." And so I did. In October, while driving to a meeting in Winston-Salem, I had a long conversation with Lauren about call discernment. Turns out she had been giving the topic lots of thought, and by the end of the conversation, I asked her to write a book that BWIM could use in future college retreats. And twenty-seven-year-old Lauren said, "Yes." It was a leap of faith for both of us.

Wait for it. I am almost to the best back story part.

Lauren was still living in Denver. She was working for a start-up company, but she had some flexibility in her schedule. So a few weeks later I called Meredith and said, "We need to go to Denver to see Lauren and plot out this book." And Meredith replied, "Well, I have some money left in my budget this year, so we need to go in December." Seriously. "Let's go in December." A few weeks later, instead of taking my vacation time before Christmas, I boarded a plane to Denver. Lauren met us at the airport and drove us to our hotel, and the three of us spent the next forty-eight hours outlining a book, this book.

And here it is . . . the best back story ever.

The morning after our arrival the three of us made a trip to Target, bought markers and paper and Scotch tape. We settled into my hotel room. We dreamed and talked and laughed and sat silently. We wrote notes on pieces of paper and taped them to the wall. We were so focused that when there was a knock on the door mid-morning, all three of us were rather startled. Lauren was sitting nearest the door so she walked over and opened it. There stood the hotel housekeeper, wanting to service my room. Lauren told her that we were working, and I called out that the room was fine, no worries about coming back. We went back to work. Writing, outlining, throwing out ideas. About an hour later there was another knock on the door, louder and harder this time. The housekeeper again, we all said. Lauren again went to the door and opened it.

And this really happened.

There standing before her was a ginormous SWAT riot shield and three SWAT officers, two of whom were holding enormous, mammoth, colossal, so big-they-didn't-look-real automatic rifles, and those guns were pointed right at Lauren.

I was sitting in the desk chair with a clear view. I saw the guns. They looked plastic, almost like toys, but they also looked seriously scary. Meredith was sitting on the bed. I don't know what kind of

view she had. But I think she caught on pretty quickly to the serious-
ness of the moment.

One of the officers demanded, "Is John Doe in this room?"[1] And
Lauren, brave Lauren, said, "Umm. No." Then the officer said to her,
"Please step out of the room into the hallway." Then he invited me
to join her, and Meredith walked behind me into the hall. Two of the
officers proceeded to search my room—looking behind the shower
curtain, under the bed, in the closet, behind the curtains. And when
they were satisfied that John Doe was not in my room, they retreated
and said "All clear." Then they began gathering up their stuff—the
riot shield and doorbanger thing (which I had not even seen until the
officer bent over to pick it up).

Being the inquisitive and easily frightened by ginormous weapons
kind of person that I am, I spoke up, "Um . . . so who is John Doe?"
And that was the only time those officers hesitated. One of them
finally spoke up and said, "Oh he is a really, really bad guy." We had
already figured that one out. And then one of us, maybe it was Meredith, said something like, "So why did you think he was here in this
room?" The tallest officer replied, "We got a tip that he was in an area
hotel in room 312. But obviously, it isn't this room or this hotel. It is
probably a different hotel." That is when I spoke up again and said,
"Are we safe? Should we change hotels? Should I get a different room?"
And the shorter officer replied, "Oh no, ma'am. You are perfectly
safe." Then they were gone. They walked away. No more explanations.
Just gone.

While outlining this book with Lauren and Meredith, my hotel
room was raided by a SWAT team in Denver. I told you—the best
back story of a book ever.

The three of us stood in the hall for a moment and then went
back in the room and sat down. Being a verbal processor, I started
talking: "How could this have happened? Did you all see how big
those guns were? What would have happened if Lauren hadn't
answered the door? What if we had just called out and said, 'No
thanks. We don't need room service?' What if those SWAT guys had
banged the door open and come in and started shooting. We could

all be dead. And Lauren. They pointed their guns at Lauren! They could have shot her."

Meanwhile, Meredith was googling John Doe, trying to figure out who this really, really bad guy was, and all the while, she was laughing—inappropriately laughing—at every question I asked. I kept saying to her, "This isn't funny." And she replied, "This is how I react to scary stuff." And Lauren, sweet Lauren, looked at both us in quiet amazement, still in shock, I think. After ten or fifteen minutes, I finally said, "We have to get out of here. I really need to get out of this room. Let's go to lunch." And so we did.

I learned several important lessons that day. First and foremost is that SWAT officers are not equipped in the area of pastoral care. They didn't stay to comfort us or even seem too concerned about how badly they had scared us. Second, reactions to fear surely are individualized. The three of us reacted so differently, and we remember the story differently. But since I am the one who is writing this foreword, I get to tell my version! Third, despite the SWAT team interruption, our outlining of a book in a hotel room in Denver worked! You hold proof in your hands—the outcome of our dreaming and sharing.

That leap of faith that I took turned out better than I even imagined. Following our time in Denver in December 2013, Lauren got busy writing, crafting together stories from her pilgrimage to Santiago and her journey toward rethinking calling. New chapters to her life and to her book emerged along the way. Just a month after Meredith and I visited her in Denver, Lauren married her sweetheart, David Bass, and just nine months or so later, she and David accepted an assignment from the Cooperative Baptist Fellowship to serve as field personnel in Cambodia. She will soon have new funny and insightful stories to add to her collection.

While the idea for this book began with an interest in college students thinking about vocational calling, the finished product has value beyond that original vision. All of us—college students, seminarians, young and new ministers, seasoned clergy, and lay people— need to read and hear Lauren's words. Her beautiful weaving together of her stories with God's story offers wisdom for those on the journey.

One of my favorite authors, Parker Palmer wrote these words: "Some journeys are direct, and some are circuitous; some are heroic, and some are fearful and muddled. But every journey, honestly undertaken, stand a chance of taking us toward the place where our deep gladness meets the world's deep need."[2] My heart is thankful for Lauren's journey, for her honesty and authenticity in sharing, and for all that is to come in the next season of her life.

Notes

1. I obviously changed the name of the really bad man. I have this odd fear that if I used his real name, he might pick up this book on call discernment one day, read about himself, and hunt me down in Atlanta.

2. Parker Palmer, *Let Your Life Speak: Listening for the Voice of Vocation* (San Francisco: Jossey-Bass, 2000) 36.

Preface

During the commencement speech at my graduate school, I was challenged to be a lifelong learner. I not only remember the challenge; I accepted it.

I love learning. I love the challenge and the rush that come from discovering and mastering new things. I am always reading, and even when I am doing laundry or commuting to work, I listen to podcasts on everything from science to economics. I am also a lover of random facts and of languages—no matter how terrible I am at learning them.

Acquiring new knowledge and skills energizes me, but I also like the actual process of learning. Going from oblivious to savvy can be a thrill. The process of learning opens many new windows into the world and into myself. The struggle, challenge, and sometimes heartbreak involved in learning pays off in new understanding and occasionally even mastery. I love that process.

For me, however, there is more to my commitment to lifelong learning than loving the process. I am committed to lifelong learning because it seems to take me close to a lifetime to truly absorb anything. I wish I were the kind of person who could take a lesson at face value and then integrate it into my life. I wish I could quickly live into abstract concepts. I wish I could know something without holding it in my hands, breathing in its smell, and tasting it. But I can't. I have to live *into* ideas. I need to test an idea's couch cushions, plopping down on each one to see how they feel under my weight. I have to be able to live with ideas for a while.

In my experience, I have learned to live into ideas through metaphors. Metaphors bring the abstract down to a level that I can poke at. Metaphors add color to abstract ideas. They shade and give dimension. I need metaphors like a painter needs paint. Metaphors allow me to hold ideas in my hands and turn them around. Metaphors open the door to ideas and invite me in. But even then, I am often slow. Maybe I am too inquisitive simply to embrace a metaphor without testing it. Maybe I am too slow on the uptake to understand it immediately. More likely, I am simply too stubborn to readily accept a metaphor.

For all my stubbornness, God seems to look with generosity on my inability to understand. God has often allowed me to live *inside* metaphors. This is a lot of work, but it is often the only way I truly learn. I can now look back and see God's generosity, albeit somewhat humorous, in the three semesters' worth of undergraduate ceramics classes I took. The classes had nothing to do with my major, yet I signed up. I haven't touched clay in years, but to this day I remember what wet clay feels like, spinning through my hands, finally centered and ready to be pulled and molded into something useful. I know that feeling. Moreover, when Isaiah says, "We are the clay, you are the potter; we are all the work of your hand" (64:8), I know that feeling, too. I understand because week after week, semester after semester, I walked back to my dorm room covered in dust, with pieces of mud in my hair. I got my hands dirty and got the chance to live inside the metaphor of God as potter and people as clay. Now I understand it.

God's generosity is behind the dirt and compost in my fingernails as I dig in my eight-by-eight-foot garden plot, which houses seeds that have become terribly sad tomato plants and triumphant cucumber vines.

God's humorous generosity is also in this vulnerable work of sitting down and writing, shaping, and seeing words become a book. God's generosity in my slowness of uptake has driven me to forty-two countries and, after I wandered around in the desert for a while, onto a path that was five hundred miles long, walked for centuries by millions before me.

Allowing us to live into metaphors is a model God has used since the beginning. God, our creator, understands that we need to see and experience things in real time and space. Adam and Eve had dirt under their fingernails as they learned the lessons of life and gardening back in the beginning. Jacob wrestled with his hands and walked the rest of his life with a physical limp.

The prophets of the Old Testament vividly understood what it meant to live into metaphors. Hosea married a prostitute; Isaiah wore a wooden yoke on his back; and Ezekiel made clay villages, baked with cow dung, and laid on his side for over a year.

Then, in the New Testament, there was Mary, who grew a child inside her for nine months and gave birth to our God with skin on. John lived in the wild, eating bugs. The disciples hiked mountains and fished with Jesus, learning about their callings along the way. My journey into my understanding calling involved a metaphor, too. Like Abraham's, my journey into my calling involved a long walk.

Calling is a broad and important concept. I have tried to understand it and live into it all my life. Abstract ideas are better than nothing, but they never get me outside my head. On top of that, listening to other people's stories of being called from point A to point B, with all the steps lining up like a staircase in between, has only left me confused and insecure about my own calling, which has surely not played out in a straight line.

Over time, I learned that I was not the only one who felt confused by my calling or had no clue how it would work out. I found fellow strugglers, and together we talked about what being called meant to us. We had to get through a lot of disappointment, confusion, and frustration first, especially those of us who had struggled with other people's limited definitions of calling. Some of us had only heard calling used in reference to the lives of preachers or missionaries. Some of us had only seen calling segregated by gender. Some of us had a hard time imagining beyond what we knew.

When we were able to step past our limits and engage our imagination and senses, we talked about what it felt like to live with and to live inside our own callings. Interestingly, as we expressed our understanding of these callings, we used metaphors to try to describe them.

For some, their calling was "stacking blocks" or the "X on the treasure map." For others, it was the "germination of a seed" or the "act of gardening." Calling was "pregnancy and birth"—the patient, loving, energy-consuming, sometimes painful work of allowing something to grow inside us and spur us into action. Calling was a "stream in the wasteland" or "Peter Pan's shadow"—the part of ourselves that might one day join us and move with us but that currently eludes us.

Calling was a "baseball game" that required patience, attention, and participation, whether from the outfield or from the bench. It was a "fondue pot" that cooks and flavors everything. It was a "deep center" and "a uniform to put on."

Calling was "learning a foreign language" or being an "immigrant" in a new and unfamiliar land. It was finding "the center of a tangled ball of yarn." It was "a statue" being chiseled or "a masterpiece" being painted, both looking different at each stage.

Calling. The concept became too rich for one-dimensional ideas. It was too important for sitting still. For me, calling is many things, but first and foremost I understand my calling as a pilgrimage. Calling is a long walk—over mountains and over plains and then over more mountains. Calling is a sacred journey taken on foot.

How did I live into the metaphor of calling as pilgrimage? Like most things in my life, I did it the hard way. I lived into the metaphor of pilgrimage by taking one. In April 2010, I embarked on the Camino de Santiago and took a five-hundred-mile walk that lasted more than a month.

In Spanish, a *camino* is a *way*, a *path*, or a *trail*. It comes from the verb *caminar*, which means *to walk*. For centuries, people have been walking from their homes all over Europe to the western corner of Spain, aiming for the city of Santiago, which was named after Saint James. Saint James evangelized Spain but was later beheaded in Jerusalem. Yet, according to legend, his remains mysteriously reappeared in western Spain, and eventually his relics were placed in a cathedral in the city named after him.

For over a thousand years, Christians have made pilgrimages to the city of Santiago. By the Middle Ages, more than half a million pilgrims were walking the paths, or *caminos*, to Santiago each year. The pilgrimage had become one of the world's most important destinations for Christians, eclipsed only by Jerusalem and Rome.

While the journey for most early pilgrims began at their front door, several main walking routes soon developed. These routes connect main cities and use old paths that were once Roman roads or

Celtic byways. Kings and clergy built hospitals, roads, bridges, churches, and hostels along these paths to aid pilgrims. The main paths are still in use today.

While the number of pilgrims on the Camino de Santiago has fluctuated through the years, dropping due to plagues, the Protestant Reformation, and religious wars, the Camino was never abandoned. In the last few decades, the Camino has again begun to attract hundreds of thousands of pilgrims each year. The paths are full once more, and they remain largely unchanged.

While some European pilgrims still begin their pilgrimages at their front doors, most pilgrims start near Spain's northeastern border with France. In total, the journey from the Spanish border to Santiago is about eight hundred kilometers, or five hundred miles. Markers are placed along the Camino, updating pilgrims on how many more kilometers they have to walk before they arrive in Santiago.

Throughout Spain, the various paths of the Camino are marked with yellow arrows or scallop shells, both symbols of the Camino. Markers guide pilgrims through countrysides full of vineyards, through the centers of major cities, and through countless small towns that were built in medieval times. Sometimes the Camino meanders through forests, and other times it parallels major freeways. Occasionally, the Camino splits and offers pilgrims a choice of paths that will rejoin later in the day or later in the week.

While modern hotels are now found all over Spain, most pilgrims rely on the same method of accommodation as pilgrims have for centuries. Pilgrim hostels, or *albergues*, dot the towns along the entire route. These hostels, sometimes run by a city or by the local parish, are typically basic, dorm-style accommodations. Some look like gymnasiums full of bunk beds, some are modern buildings, and others are converted Romanesque monasteries.

The hostels are reserved for pilgrims. Guests are typically asked to leave a small donation or to pay a fee that is usually between five to ten dollars for an overnight stay. Accommodations vary widely from hostel to hostel. Most hostels have kitchens, and some offer a communal meal in the evening. Some have clothes washers and dryers. A few have curfews and mandatory "lights out" hours. The only guarantee is snoring pilgrims.

Modern pilgrims come in all ages and nationalities. They walk for all kinds of reasons and represent all stages of faith. Some pilgrims have the best experience of their lives, and others cry their way to Santiago. Regardless of their differences, all pilgrims who make it to the moss-covered plaza of Santiago return home changed.

I was no different. This is the story of my calling and my pilgrimage.

Chapter 1

Villa Franca– Qué Quieres?

Qué quieres, Lorena? Qué quieres? I repeated it to myself as I stared at my reflection in the window of an almost thousand-year-old church. Often at my most desperate, most joyful, most frustrated moments, I turn to the remnants of Spanish that still cling to my mind's bones. *What do you want, Lauren? What do you actually want to do with yourself? What do you want?*

I had already walked more than five hundred kilometers, or more than three hundred miles, from Pamplona, and that day had trekked twenty-three kilometers to the city of Villa Franca, but I left my bag at the hostel and slipped away, alone, into the rainy town and walked some more. I found myself at the Church of Santiago on a hill at the edge of town. The church, built in the twelfth century and still hundreds of kilometers from the city of Santiago, was given permission by Catholic authorities to grant pilgrims too sick to continue the journey the same indulgence and pardon as those who traveled all the way to the moss-covered cathedral in Santiago.

The church was closed, but I huddled under the awning of the Door of Forgiveness, the door that sick pilgrims passed through to officially receive their pardon. I tried to stay dry from the sudden increase in rain. I had walked over mountains and made it across the draining and solitary plains. But here I was, more than two-thirds of the way through my pilgrimage, and all I could do was walk around town, my feet aching and blistered, trying to outrun the suffocating realization that I *still* had no idea what I wanted.

Qué quieres? I stood on that doorstep and for a while looked outward at the mountains and the clouds rolling in from the south.

I finally turned and looked at my reflection in the glass of the church window. *What do you want, Lauren?*

If I could have said what I wanted, I am such a make-it-work kind of woman that I could have gotten myself on the right path immediately. But what do I want? What do I want to do with myself? With my life?

The honest answer was silence. I did not know.

I could start my story, my journey, at the beginning—excited to meet Claire, my first pilgrim friend, on day one. Or I could start my telling at the end, triumphant in the plaza of Santiago de Compostela. Yet the story of my pilgrimage, and the story of my calling, has much more in common with this rainy day on the steps of that tiny Romanesque church staring into my reflection. Because that remains the question: Lauren, what do you want?

I keep asking it. Occasionally, I think I know the answer. I think I find a job or a position or a city that works. I think *this is it*. Then the suffocation comes. The AmeriCorps term runs out, and I am back to sending résumés into the void. A job turns progressively toxic. Restlessness sets in, and I need to get a move on, but again I don't know where to go.

I always come back to that frustratingly core and unknown place where I ask myself, *What do you want? What were you made to do? What will satisfy you? Why are there so many misses in your search? Where is the target that keeps moving? What is your calling?*

I want to know what I want, what I am called to do, so I can get on with it already. I want to make it work. I want to change lives. I want to do something I love *and* pay the bills, even if just barely. What was I made for? Someone just tell me, and I will get busy.

I have good intentions about being patient with my calling and my journey. Really, I do. I just get a bit frantic sometimes. When I find myself job searching yet again, when I have no idea where I should move next, when the position I thought could be life-giving for me becomes otherwise, when I start calculating how long until I graduate and then how long I've been *out* of grad school, when I feel like my purpose is slipping through my fingers, I get unsettled.

I panic. Before I know it, I get sucked into *ugly-faced cries*. (You probably know the kinds of cries I'm talking about.)

I'm not sure why this path is such a hard one for me or why it's so hard for so many people I love who are walking the same journey of calling. Why can't we find the right road? I don't know. What do we want? I don't know. Will people even let us do it when we figure it out? I don't know.

I'll go ahead and say it: my path of calling, of sorting myself out, has already been a long journey. I have walked a journey that has felt like miles and miles over mountains on blistered feet. Other people seem to have different experiences. Some people feel called to something specific, at a young age even, and their whole lives lead up to that career or position or vocation. From point A straight to point B, with numbered steps along the way. Others seem to walk happily enough through their lives, without giving a second's thought to what their calling might be. I don't fall into either of those categories.

Originally, I did think I was going to have a point A to point B kind of calling. After a childhood of studying missionaries in my good Southern Baptist Girls in Action classes, I felt God tug at me, and I knew what my calling must be. I was going to be a missionary! It made sense. I would take a slow boat to China, or I would be like the missionaries who showed slides of Africans dancing and singing in Swahili.

At the age of twelve, I walked down the aisle of my home church, and the big, kind man who was our interim pastor at the time shook my hand. I turned toward the congregation in my purple polka-dotted dress, and he told the congregation that I had *surrendered to the call*. Everyone was pleased and not too surprised. I already had a deep love for learning about other cultures, so most of the people I knew accepted my calling without hesitation or much thought. My mom was the only one who put a caveat on my calling. "Just be open to go wherever God leads you," she said. I thought she was simply uneasy with the thought of her youngest child and only daughter sailing on a slow boat to China. It turns out, however, that my mom, all those years ago, gave me some of the best advice anyone has ever given me about calling. Yet, while hers was good advice, it does not necessarily lead one toward a point A to point B kind of calling. I thought that being open to go wherever God led me would take me to a plan. Instead, this advice has led to lots of dusty roads, blisters, ugly cry faces, and standing alone in front of church windows, asking myself, *What you are doing? What do you want?*

This is how I got to that church in Villa Franca, staring at my reflection, and what happened afterward. What follows is the story of how I took my life and my search for calling seriously enough to strap on a backpack and hiking boots and hit the trail. What I learned walking across Spain forever changed the way I look my life and my calling.

Chapter 2

Pamplona–Getting Lost and Getting Started

The beginning was a bit rough. I had not made many preparations for the Camino ahead of time. Just getting to Pamplona, where I had decided to start my pilgrimage, included a taxi, a bus, a plane, a train, two more buses, and a two-hour walk with all my belongings on my back.

My pilgrimage along the Camino de Santiago was a part of a larger trip I was taking. Finding myself burnt out and with a stash of frequent-flyer miles and a savings account that I had labeled "Sabbatical," I decided to plan and take an almost yearlong break. Planning a yearlong sabbatical was overwhelming, so in the end, I broke my trip into regions of the world where I wanted to travel. From there, I decided to buy only the plane tickets that I would need to travel between regions, plan the first two weeks of the first portion, and then figure the rest out as I went. One thing I knew for sure was that I wanted to walk the Camino de Santiago. So I bought plane tickets.

I would fly into Girona, just outside of Barcelona, late on April 1 and make my way to Pamplona. I would fly out of Santiago on May 18. That would give me about six weeks to get from Pamplona to Santiago, or beyond, on foot. I really had no idea how fast I would walk. Actually, there were lots of details I did not know about the Camino. I had read through many online forums in which former and upcoming pilgrims asked questions and gave advice. I had read half a book about the Camino. But all the advice overwhelmed me. Simply trying to decide which pair of hiking boots to buy nearly exhausted the mental resources I had for planning.

Knowing that I can plan myself to death, I cut back on my research. I told myself I would figure out the essentials of the Camino and then, as with the rest of my sabbatical, figure out the other details on the fly. I decided to start in Pamplona, which was the easiest city to get to along the beginning portion of the Camino de Santiago. I downloaded a brief guide to the Camino that only listed the distances between the cities that I would pass through and the hostels along the way. I decided that once I got to Pamplona, I would buy the extra things I needed at a sporting goods store in town and mail everything but the essentials in my backpack to Santiago. I would then be able to reclaim my "stuff" once I arrived in Santiago and my walking was done. I booked a small room just off the Camino in Pamplona so the only thing I would have to do to begin the Camino on my first day would be to walk out the door.

My plan seemed simple.

As it turned out, my plan was a little too simple for Spain. Prepared for a day of shopping and running errands in Pamplona, I quickly realized that I had planned my errand day on a Sunday. Errands simply do not happen on Sundays in Spain. Nothing is open. Instead of running around town preparing, I went to a nearby church for a service and spent the morning eating *churros y chocolate*. I decided that if I was going to walk across an entire peninsula, one more day of rest and a little fried dough were probably not going to hurt me.

On Monday, my errands went better than I expected. I picked up a small sleeping bag, a cheap raincoat, a waterproof cover for my backpack, and, mostly for my dad's sake, a safety whistle. (I had been advised to get a whistle so that if I got hurt or fell in a ditch along the way, someone might hear me and find me after my voice had given out. In the end, I never got around to taking the whistle out of the packaging.) As planned, I mailed all the nonessentials to Santiago. In a hopeful turn of events, I even got a friendly Spanish postal worker.

Free from most of my belongings and cheered by my accomplished errands, I needed one more thing to get myself started on the path to Santiago. I went to the cathedral to get my pilgrim's "credentials." Sometimes the credentials are called a pilgrim's passport. The credentials are little booklets distributed by the Catholic Church, and, like passports, they have space in them for pilgrims to store stamps from their journey. Pilgrim hostels, churches, cathedrals, and other sites along the way have stamps that pilgrims can collect to prove that they are actually pilgrims and that they have traveled as far as they say they have. When pilgrims arrive in Santiago, church officials look through a pilgrim's credentials to authenticate his or her journey.

So on that Monday, I walked through downtown Pamplona toward the cathedral. Passing flowerbeds full of tulips and statues of Hemingway, I walked a route that holds markers for both the Camino de Santiago and the *encierro*, Pamplona's famous running of the bulls. Once I got to the city's cathedral, I was excited to complete my first real pilgrim act.

And the door was locked.

I walked around to another door of the cathedral and found it locked as well. I made a full loop around the building. All the doors were locked. So much for my passport. Not wanting to give up my good mood or delay my start, I decided to pick up my passport at the church in Puente de la Reina at the end of my first day on the trail. I headed back to my rented room, took everything out of my backpack for one last inventory, packed it up again, pulled down the blinds, and tried to sleep.

The next morning, I woke up with a smile on my face. I let out a tiny squeal while still in bed and was ready to go only a few minutes later. My bag was packed, I had slept in my pilgrim clothes, and the night before I had laid out my breakfast banana and snacks for the first day. I slathered some precautionary IcyHot onto my fickle ankles, put on my fancy hiking socks, and carefully tied my boots. I stretched. I drank a glass of water. I folded the map of Pamplona and put it in my pocket. I strapped on my backpack and walked out the door.

I walked toward the university, strutting past the college students on their way to class. I was off to join the official Camino path. It felt so right. I stopped to take a picture of my shadow walking along the Camino.

I soon realized, though, that I was not on the Camino at all. In fact, I was walking east instead of west. The road I was on should have connected with the Camino, but it hadn't. I backtracked. No sign of the Camino. My smiley excitement started to look a bit more like panic. *I can't even* find *the Camino.*

Anyone who knows me knows that I am directionally challenged. This fact is no secret, and getting lost was one of my biggest fears about walking the Camino (right next to my very real concern of getting bedbugs). I can get exceptionally lost just about anywhere. I am easily turned around and disoriented. Unfortunately, I also have a tendency to think that I am going in the right direction. My instinct is always to keep going and see if the way I'm headed turns out to be the right road. Before smart phones, my mom would get calls from me and have to patiently explain that I had gone sixty miles in the wrong direction.

So here I was, on my first day of walking the Camino, stuck on the outskirts of one of Spain's major cities. I was lost. I could not even find the place to start. I had no idea where the path began—the one I was going to follow through the countryside and mountains for eight hundred kilometers. My future on the Camino was looking grim.

I pulled out my map. The road on which I was walking back and forth should have connected with the road that the Camino followed on its way out of the city. But I could not find the place where the two roads connected. As I studied the map, it eventually clicked. The road the Camino followed was *under* the road where I was walking back and forth. The paths looked like they would merge, but I had missed the Camino because I was walking along a road that went *over* it via an overpass.

Finally, I found the overpass I needed. I spotted the path the Camino followed below it. There was no sidewalk or even a path for me to get to the road below. I calculated my options. As soon as there weren't *too* many people around, I darted through the hedges along the road and carefully jogged and skidded down the hill to the lower road. The sidewalks had small, metal shells imbedded into them every ten feet or so. Scalloped shells, or *conchas*, are symbols of Santiago.

I was on the Camino at last.

Little did I know, these starts and stops would characterize my entire Camino. Even more so, these starts and stops have come to characterize my entire journey into my calling. During my teens and early twenties, I had a fairly clear and not very complicated idea of what my calling was or, perhaps better stated, what my calling *would* be. My calling story started out like most classic calling stories, even if it did not progress like those classic calling stories are supposed to.

Like many people before me, I had walked down an aisle or two. I had shaken hands with ministers. I had even gone to seminary. After seminary, though, it finally became apparent that no matter how hard I tried, my calling was not headed in the direction that I thought it would when I was that seventh grade girl in a purple polka-dotted dress. Everyone in the church, from my Sunday school teachers to my grandmother, had visions of me spending my entire adult life in China or Africa. I was *called to missions*, and at the time that was what missions looked like to seventh graders and septuagenarians alike.

None of us realized that I would not be like Lottie Moon, famed Baptist missionary who gave her life, literally, to ministry in China. She felt called, rode a boat to China, and stayed there. She learned the language, absorbed the culture, and loved the people. Eventually, during a time of severe famine, Lottie gave away so much of her own meager amounts of food to aid the Chinese people she loved that she ended up dying of starvation herself.

Growing up with the lore of these great missionaries, and limited examples of women being *called* into any other kind of ministry, I have gone through times in which I have longed for a forgotten corner of the world of my own to hole up in, give the rest of my life to, and get down to the business of *ministry*.

The congregants who affirmed this calling in me, the same ones who also watched and affirmed my baptism, had no way of knowing then what I myself did not know—that the calling bubbling up inside me would take me on a winding journey through refugee communities in west Texas to high school English classes in Europe and to doling out rental assistance and bologna sandwiches in a basement in downtown Denver, Colorado. None of these places or tasks were what any of us thought would unfold for me. But maybe, just maybe, these "odd" places and tasks were my calling after all.

At times, with a big sigh, I remember what was such a hard lesson for me—that the calling I have received, like all callings, is a calling that moves. My calling is one that requires waiting like the Israelites did with only pillars of cloud and fire, but my calling also insists that I be ready to move when the cloud lifts. It demands that I learn how to be present without getting too settled. My calling requires movement, but sometimes it also requires *churros y chocolate*.

In my pilgrimage of calling, I find myself often on the move. I have found myself walking back and forth between gardening with people experiencing homelessness—picking flowers or bowls of spinach—and answering phone calls as an office manager.

This calling of mine did not come with an easy blueprint or a straightforward title. There is no job security. There is no prestige. There is no one to hand me credentials. I often wonder if the path that I am traveling can even be called "ministry." I sometimes question whether the path I am on is my calling at all.

But when I stop and get my bearings, I occasionally see it. I spot my calling and have to dart through the bushes and scamper down the hills of overpasses. There are days when I want another path. Sometimes I wish I had one that was clearer, easier. Other times I just want a calling to ministry that "looks like ministry." I want a job, a title, and a paycheck that is a few degrees of separation further away from minimum wage. I want anything that will give me an identity to hold up and hide behind.

There are days when I crave validation in my calling and in my ministry. *Someone please tell me that I am headed in the right direction, that I am on the right path, that this is ministry.*

Those starts and stops, those uncertain lost moments, make up the truth about my calling. I thought that I was being called onto a boat to sail to a foreign country (or some variation of that theme). I thought I would learn a language and dish out big pots of soup while wearing native garb. I thought my denomination would support me with the title *missionary* and give me enough money to buy rice and cloth that could be sewn into clothes. I thought little Girls in Action groups would celebrate my birthday and send me packets of hand-written cards and chewing gum.

The simple expectations with which I began my journey gave me a false impression of where I would end up. They even sent me down some wrong paths and back again. I had gotten lost and started in the wrong direction. I had thought that I was headed one way, but as it turned out, I was indeed headed in another.

Those expectations, though, with the Holy Spirit nudging me, keep pushing me toward the path of my calling. Throughout the years following my calling, I have been excited, and I have been confused. I have been surefooted and walking due east, in precisely the wrong direction, and I have also walked on a path that was marked clearly as the right one for me.

In my Camino and in my journey into my calling, just getting started was messy and a lot more work than I anticipated. My beginnings were representative of the whole of my Camino and my calling. That first day would not be the last time I got lost or went in the wrong direction. It surely would not be the last time I looked every-where for where to go next without realizing my path was right under my feet. Yet, looking back at those beginnings, I realize that while it was bumpy and confusing, I found the path of my calling in the end.

I have discovered that how we find the path of our calling is not the important piece of the puzzle. We might discover the path of our calling in a seminary class, in conversations with passengers on a city bus, or while walking toward Santiago. We might find the path of our calling in the seventh grade or a decade into retirement. We might be male, or we might be female. We might stutter or stumble or walk a mile in the wrong direction before we figure out the way to go. We might be skipping with excitement or on the edge of a cliff of tears. It does not matter.

What matters is finding the path, sorting out which way is west, and starting to walk.

Chapter 3

Buscando Flechas– Finding the Path as I Go

There is no limit to the preparation that pilgrims can do before they start walking the Camino. Plenty of guidebooks in plenty of languages will tell as much as you would like to know. The guidebooks describe the trail, the towns and cities, the food and flowers, and the history. The detail all of the route and hostel options and provide the mileage and elevation change for each stage of the Camino.

I was overwhelmed with the information.

I'm a researcher by nature. I research everything, trying to get the best deals at the grocery store, the healthiest and most nutritious food, and the best hotel or hostel in whatever city I am going to next. I can obsess over these things. When it came time for me to do the work of planning my own wedding, I was lost in a sea of research for practically every single detail.

All this research can, of course, be exhausting. I end up becoming an expert in lots of random, small fields, such as which yogurt brand has the most protein per ounce, per dollar, or the best way to amend the soil in my garden. I also end up spending a significant amount of time and energy making even the smallest decisions. Larger decisions can leave me in a flood of sticky notes, filled with pros and cons and crippling indecisiveness. I want to know my choices, and I want to know the possible outcomes. I want to choose the best option.

Thankfully, when it came time for me to plan for the Camino de Santiago, I was simply unable to put the kind of time and energy into preparing for the trip that I put into other areas of my life. I had just finished graduate school and returned from a semester of cross-cultural ministry with refugees in Belgium. The semester fulfilled my final seminary credit, got me out of west Texas, and taught me lots of lessons, but by the end of it, I was more exhausted than energized. And in the midst of my exhaustion, I was busy planning my sabbatical and getting ready to leave the country for the rest of the year within a few weeks.

I had plane tickets to buy, hostels to book, and many travel decisions to make (Albania or Jordan? Nicaragua or Guatemala? A month or a week there? Hotel or hostel?). I was all over travel message boards and the travel section of Barnes and Noble. When I turned my attention to the Camino portion of my sabbatical, I was thoroughly exhausted *and* relieved.

I wanted to give the Camino and my preparation to walk it the same kind of in-depth research that I gave to my apartment search, or at least the same kind of research I gave to choosing the right vitamin brand. I did discover information about how to pace myself on the Camino, what kind of boots to buy and how to break them in, and how to prepare physically for the hike. Yet I knew that the Camino did not need to be researched and planned to the nth degree.

After all, this freedom from constant planning is part of what drew me to time on the Camino. You don't actually even need a map to walk to Santiago. While there's more information printed about the Camino than even I could absorb, all you really need to do to make it to Santiago is walk westward and keep your eyes open.

The Camino has been walked for almost a thousand years, and it is marked simply. Arrows guide pilgrims the entire way. Usually yellow, these arrows are embedded into the street tiles in the downtowns of cities. Arrows are found on small concrete markers throughout the countryside. Previous pilgrims have gathered rocks and arranged them into arrows in the mountains to help future pilgrims avoid confusion at diverging paths. It is said that all pilgrims have to do in order to make it to Santiago is *buscar flechas*, or search for arrows.

For once my plan was simple. I'd given myself plenty of time to make it to Santiago before my flight out of Spain. There was no need to hurry or keep to a schedule. For my duration of time on the Camino, in a radically simple shift, all I had to do each morning was wake up, walk west, and follow arrows. When I got tired, I would stop for the night in the nearest town.

While I did download a basic guide that told me which cities along the way had overnight accommodations, and the distance between them, the method of relying solely on arrows and other pilgrims worked. At intersections, arrows were spray painted on the sidewalks, and concrete markers dotted the countryside with tile arrows. All I had to do was watch those yellow arrows.

I wish the path of my calling were as well marked as the Camino. At times I feel, see, or hear firm directors of my calling and purpose, but those moments are rare. *Buscando flechas*, or looking for arrows, is sometimes much harder on the path to calling than on the path to Santiago.

Looking for arrows on the Camino and pointers on the journey into my calling both require constant awareness. At times on the Camino, usually when I was deep in thought, conversation, or mud, I would miss arrows. I would walk painful miles, alone, in the wrong direction. I felt confident walking when reassuring arrows appeared every five minutes or so. Even an arrow every twenty minutes still felt comfortable. But if an hour passed without an arrow, I started to get uneasy. The feeling that I was lost, headed in the wrong direction, crept up on me.

I have felt the same way about my calling again and again. When people are weekly or monthly, or even just quarterly, speaking words of affirmation and guidance into my calling and vocation, I walk on confidently. When I have a job, when writing is going well, when people ask me to take on leadership roles, or when I see even small fruit from my labor, I feel like I am on the correct path. When words come easily for me or when my efforts seem to be sending me in the right direction, I walk on.

Other times when following my calling, however, I have no clue where I am or in which direction I am headed. I can't even remember when I last saw an arrow. Sometimes I feel like I'm headed west, in the right general direction, but sometimes I can't even tell where the sun is setting. I don't know whether I should keep marching forward into the unknown, potentially putting myself further behind and further off the right path, or if I should just admit defeat and turn around.

Where are those arrows?

As I have journeyed into my calling, I have experienced all sides of this equation. At times I hit a dead end. At times I was walking the wrong way but made it to where I was going after all. Other times I marched on, unsure as ever, into unmarked territory, and realized it was exactly were I was supposed to be.

My graduate school journey in west Texas felt a lot like the latter. I'd marched myself right up to my last month of undergraduate studies with no idea what I would do afterward. I was undecided and conflicted. I'd taken the year before off to live and teach English in Spain, and at the end of my teaching contract, I was relieved to know I had to return to Texas to finish my one remaining semester of college while many of my friends struggled to decide whether to renew their contracts and teach another year in Spain, take jobs back in their hometowns, or join the Peace Corps.

I was relieved that my next step was mapped out. What I hadn't anticipated was just how quickly I would be midway through that final semester without having given much thought to what would come next. Graduating in December meant that I didn't even have the luxury of a summer to figure out my next move.

I thought about my choices. I thought about where I wanted to be long term. I made Venn diagrams and talked to friends and mentors. I still had no idea what I was supposed to do.

One of my choices was to stay in west Texas and attend graduate school at the seminary affiliated with my university. I knew and liked many of the professors and felt certain that I could get some kind of scholarship. But I wasn't sure that seminary, especially seminary for three or four more years in *west Texas,* would be right or sustainable for my newly transformed, world-traveling heart. Was staying in Texas settling? Was it smart? Would it be suffocating? Did my "calling to missions" obligate me to choose seminary so I could get through training and get on with my calling afterward?

I had no idea.

I looked for clues everywhere. I finally stumbled upon what I took for an arrow before I even knew what it meant to *buscar flechas*. A pastor in an even smaller west Texas town spoke on what it meant to love God with your heart, soul, *and* mind. Through that sermon, I felt a nudge toward exploring loving God with all my mind in graduate school. Eventually I felt at peace staying right where I was in west Texas to do that. I had an arrow, and I followed it.

Seminary was grueling at times. Looking back, I know some of it was my own making, my own rush to get done with it, my drive to get on with ministry and my desire to overachieve, but there were other times when it just didn't seem to *fit*. My degree was a long one, and I sometimes doubted if I would finish. I doubted if it was right for me. I wondered if I should continue.

I felt quite alone, and I wondered if I had made the right decision. Arrows grew sparse. I had started to fear that I was no longer on the right path. Fortunately, I was able to look back and feel like the arrows of the Holy Spirit had led me to that spot. I continued walking onward in faith. With hindsight, I can see that I was absolutely on the right path even though I wasn't sure at the time. The lessons I learned, a significant portion out of the classroom, and the transformation that took place in those often sleep-deprived and sometimes tear-filled years were exactly what I needed. I was on the right path in spite of my misgivings.

Occasionally, on the Camino de Santiago and on my pilgrimage into my calling, the opposite happened. I would realize I hadn't seen an arrow for a while, but I would keep moving forward. I wouldn't know it until afterward, but somewhere along the path I had gotten off track. I was not actually on the officially marked path. With God's grace, though, most of the time I made it to the city I was walking toward anyway.

Sometimes I would spot the entrance to the city from across a field and cut through a pasture, with scratches to show for it. Sometimes I would end up walking along a freeway instead of through a scenic pass. Taking the right or wrong path, though, I would somehow arrive at the correct destination. God seems to have a way of bringing us to the correct destination even when we veer off course.

Don't get me wrong; there are also times when I hit a complete dead end or cliff's edge when trying to follow my calling. For a while I wondered if perhaps my calling was better suited to the academic world than to the mission field. After all, I enjoyed learning, so I started thinking about PhD work and teaching. I researched schools and programs. I talked with both professors and friends who were in doctoral programs. Many things made that path seem like a good fit for me.

In the end, while studying for the GRE, I hit a brick wall. I was sitting at my desk making flash cards of Latin root words when I realized I was on the wrong path. I realized the GRE was just a hurdle for me to jump over and was not reflective of what it would be like to get a PhD and teach, but it all seemed wrong to me. I had followed what I thought were arrows, but they had led me to a dead end.

I closed the study book and started my hike backwards.

The same thing happened to me on my Camino.

As I approached Galicia, the final region of the Camino, the landscape turned greener and more mountainous each day. I spent the majority of the morning thinking, *This is just so beautiful.* The mountains and skies were blue and pink and green. Wild mountain roses bloomed all along the path, and I stopped every fifteen minutes to smell, pick, and tuck them behind my ear.

I'd met back up with Victoria, a young German whom I had walked with for most of the last few days. We chatted and told stories as we hiked higher and higher on the mountain. Because of the beautiful vistas and good stories, we didn't realize what had happened until it was too late.

We were lost.

We got to the top of the mountain, and there was nothing but trees and rocks. The gravel trail we were following simply stopped. There was no way forward.

We had been observant as we hiked that morning, and we had four eyes between us to spot arrows. We didn't know how we'd gotten to that dead end at the top of the mountain. We could see a town in the distance behind a couple more hills, but there was no way to get to it—no way except by turning around and going back down the way we had come up.

We hiked down the mountain, looking for the alternate trail we had missed, and finally found a small trail that branched off from our path. We realized that cyclists must have ridden over the stones, originally laid out in an arrow, and accidentally scrambled them so that they looked like a helpful barrier pushing us toward the main path instead of an arrow pointing us down the smaller trail. We arranged the jumble of rocks back into an unmistakable arrow for future pilgrims and started hiking upward again—this time on the correct path.

Backtracking can be tiring and frustrating, and sometimes it is no one's fault. It happens when we are paying attention. Every once in a while, we end up at a dead end, and there is no sane choice but to backtrack and leave those PhD programs and Peace Corps positions behind, to change majors, or to end a relationship. Sometimes it is time to go back and find the right small path.

It is painful to walk back down the same road, doubling the miles walked, just to get back to where you missed an arrow.

But what choices do we have when we hit a dead end?

I have had to realize that there isn't always a choice. Sometimes, especially when it comes to calling, and especially when it comes to a decision that researching until my hair turns gray won't solve, I want to stand in the middle of the path I am on and demand an arrow. Stubbornly, I tell myself and God that I am going to sit there until I find an arrow, until I clearly know which path is the right one. *I will sit here all day!* I say. *All year!*

I want signs. I want arrows. I want guides. I want *urim* and *thummin* and fleeces drenching wet in the morning.

I've come to realize, though, that we can stand there and look for signs or arrows all day or all year. Maybe we will spot one we didn't see at first, but otherwise, there's nothing there for us. Sometimes the path only appears when we start walking again. We have to keep walking forward and pray that we are on the right path or that God will get us to our destination, or we have to turn around and go back.

I learned both to pay attention and to relax when it came to directions on the Camino and in my calling. After painfully backtracking, whether on tired feet at the end of a long day of hiking or after months of researching PhD programs, I learned to cherish the arrows I found both on the Camino and in my journey of calling.

On the Camino, I began to look for arrows constantly as I walked. When arrows became less frequent, I came up with a plan to calm my nerves. I began to pull out the camera in my pocket to take pictures of the arrows along the trail with my watch in the same frame. That way, when I started to get nervous later, I could look back at the pictures and know exactly when I saw the last arrow.

I started to do the same with my calling. When a friend, a professor, or a pastor told me I was good at something, I often recognized it as an arrow, or as a pointer in the right direction. When a task or a relationship gave me great joy, I made note of it. When I felt the nudge of the Holy Spirit, I wrote about the experience. Later, if I got to what seemed like a forsaken destination, I could look back and know how I got there and that maybe I was in the right place.

Other times I looked at a job opening that closed without anyone ever calling me back as an arrow in another direction. I looked deeply and saw exhaustion or sickness as a nudge that something wasn't right. I took in those arrows and realized it was time for the painful but hopeful journey backwards—doubling my efforts but being guided by my mistakes and the Holy Spirit all the way back to the correct path. The process of retracing steps is tiring but renews my resolve to observe the way God is working around me.

Looking for arrows has also taught me to embrace paying attention as a spiritual discipline. Instead of keeping my head down, hand on the plow at all times, I allow myself to keep my head up. I have learned to look around, listen, and recognize both obvious and subtle signs of the Holy Spirit. I now realize that stopping to pay attention to the direction my calling is taking me is not a luxury. Paying attention is a necessity.

Embracing the spiritual discipline of paying attention allows me to spot more arrows along the way. Paying attention also allows me to see the wildflowers by the side of the road, the hints of mountains in the distance, and the pilgrims traveling further ahead of me. Instead of relying on my careful plans and research, I try to be present in each moment and each mile of the path. I stop forcing myself to make *the best* decision every time and allow the Holy Spirit to be the cloud directing me in the distance.

Finding and relying on arrows to guide me requires attention, yes, but it also allows me to relax a bit. While it didn't, and doesn't, always feel like it, not having to plan out every step of my journey or decide where to go at every intersection is a blessing. I was relieved not to have to research and plan my entire Camino or my entire calling before I began. I know now that I don't have to strategize or memorize. I just have to walk.

Calling, I've discovered, just like the Camino, is a process of following. A calling is not a prescription of a specific, ideal job, and a calling is not a career plan. A calling is a journey of paying attention, of altering course when necessary, and of relaxing.

We are not called to a plan; we are called to a path that we follow. This *path*, in the words of Spanish poet Antonio Machado, *is made by walking. There is no path,* he writes. *The path is made of your steps and nothing more* ("Proverbios y Cantares" in *Campos de Castilla,* 1912, my translation).

Chapter 4

Alto de Perdón– The Baggage We Carry

My excitement about being on the Camino, walking in the footsteps of the millions of pilgrims who came before me, carried me for the first portion of my journey. My feet were still in good shape—no soreness or blisters, not even any calluses yet—and I was sticking to the schedule I'd designed to keep myself from overdoing it. I stopped every hour to stretch and to drink water, and I took a break every two hours for a snack.

The scenery was beautiful and green, and the landscape was mostly flat. Before long, though, the flatness gave way. Because I started my pilgrimage on the other side of the Pyrenees, I came upon my first mountain outside of Pamplona. Here at *Alto de Perdón*—or, in English, Peak of Forgiveness—I learned that while at times the Camino de Santiago could go *around* mountains, it usually prefers to go right over them.

On fresh legs and in good spirits, I was undaunted. Besides, without an exhaustive guide, I didn't know I was about to hike up and over a real mountain.

The legend of this steep mountain is that by the time a pilgrim climbed all the way to the top, he would have atoned for all of his sins—thus its name, "Peak of Forgiveness." The legend didn't align well with my theology, but that didn't matter. I was relatively sure that any forgiveness I could have possibly hiked off on my way up the mountain was overshadowed by all the cursing I murmured under my breath. Specifically, I cursed the weight on my shoulders. How did my backpack get so heavy? As I hiked up and up, I mentally combed through every item in the backpack and cursed the weight of each one.

I thought I had mailed all nonessentials to Santiago before leaving Pamplona. When I started out, my backpack felt relatively empty. I thought I was packing light. But I soon realized on that steep climb that every ounce of weight matters when climbing mountains and hiking dozens of miles a day.

I eventually made it to the top of Alto de Perdón. On the way up, I stopped often to take pictures, and I hoped no one would notice that I was deeply out of breath and trying to mask that I needed a break. At the top of the mountain, a monument with bronze cutouts of pilgrims across the ages (depicted with their walking sticks and wind-blown cloaks) greets travelers. I could see for miles and miles, back to the east from which I had come and forward into the west where I was headed.

Before taking it all in, though, I slipped off my backpack and let it hit the ground. I collapsed next to it and took out my water bottle.

Rehydrated, I caught my breath and ate some cookies offered by the German pilgrim sitting next to me. As I munched, I tried to decide what to ditch from my pack that evening.

I thought I had done a good job paring down my pilgrimage gear. I knew beforehand that the weight of my backpack would matter, but I didn't understand how much even an extra bottle of water would weigh down each of my steps. Walking that long journey meant I had to be conscious of every ounce I carried in order to minimize fatigue and stress on my body. That night in the hostel, I sifted through my belongings even further.

I carried one set of clothes to sleep in while my hiking gear dried on the line outside. I brought no makeup, and I trimmed my toiletry supplies to sunscreen, lip balm, toothpaste, and shampoo (that doubled as soap and laundry detergent). I even traveled all the way to León without so much as a comb or hairbrush. In León, a big city about two-thirds of the way to Santiago, I broke down and bought myself the lightest brush in the shop as a present so that I could brush my hair, which had started to turn into dreadlocks.

I stopped carrying extra water and more snacks than I needed for the day. Instead, I filled my water bottle at fountains along the way or in the bathrooms of cafés. I bought enough food for each day and no more. If I had leftovers, I shared them rather than carrying them with me.

I've realized that sorting through the baggage we carry around in life, and especially as we journey into our callings, is just as important as carefully combing through the weight on my back on the Camino. We all have baggage—events from our past that taunt us, insecurities, fears, expectations, perceived limitations, and so on. Sometimes we don't realize the weight we carry. Other times carrying the extra weight with us seems warranted or inevitable.

Often we don't realize the implications of the weight we carry. Just like on my Camino, my baggage does not seem problematic until I am under stress. When we are at our most vulnerable, our most challenged, or our most desperate, the issues hiding in our baggage seem to get unexpectedly heavy. Our personal issues make their way out of us and spill onto others, even those we are trying to help. Unless we commit to sorting through our baggage, these past difficulties will get in the way of our finding and continuing to follow our callings.

Once I realized how, especially under stress or over time, baggage complicates life, I saw the phenomenon everywhere, especially at the top. I saw people who had been too afraid or too busy to sort through their baggage on their way to the top of businesses, organizations, governments, and churches. People in positions of authority in all sectors are susceptible to abuses of power and position. Many times these abuses happen because leaders have neglected the hard and dark inner work of dealing honestly with their baggage. The so-called "helping professions," including ministry and nonprofit work, seem to be especially dangerous places for people who have skimped on the inner work of sifting through baggage. These positions are dangerous because we easily see our own baggage in other people as we try to help them.

For example, have you ever met a pastor who grabs for power and control (usually without realizing it), who can hear potentially helpful critiques only as treason, or who can receive questions about policies only as doubts about his or her authority? Have you ever encountered ministers who use emotions to manipulate or gain control? Have you noticed nonprofit or aid workers trying to right wrongs or hurts in their personal lives through the lives of their clients or the people they serve? Have you observed lay leaders who are so plagued by insecurities that they eventually step down from their leadership roles?

Our baggage weighs us down as we try to walk out our callings, and it affects those around us. If we aren't committed to leaving some of it behind, we will hurt others, hurt ourselves, or give up. Climbing the path of our calling is too difficult if we insist on holding on to every piece of our baggage.

Overachievement has been one piece of my baggage, an aspect of my mode for operating in the world that has hindered me as I have walked into my calling. It's a piece of my baggage that stretches back decades.

In high school I participated in practically every organization and activity available. Sometimes I participated in all these things without much effort, although other times I put forth tremendous effort. Either way, I did most of them well. I was on the varsity basketball team, section leader in the band, class president, *and* valedictorian. I graduated high school with an entire year's worth of college credits under my belt.

I was also exhausted.

I was tired of doing lots of things just because I could, so I cut back when I went to college. I cut back *and* ended up graduating a semester early even though I took off my entire junior year to live and teach in Spain with a grant from the Spanish embassy. I graduated with a 4.0 grade point average. I hadn't intended to continue at such an exhausting pace, but it was a pace I knew well.

That pace propelled me forward for a while longer. I was in graduate school taking a full load of classes each semester, working three different jobs, and excelling at it all.

I'm no perfectionist. But overachiever? I have that written all over me. It's part of my baggage. If there is a bar in front of me, then I want to jump over it, no matter how high or how out of my natural skill set it hangs.

My overachieving nature is not all bad. Overachievement has led me to where I am now. It has trained me over the years to take on difficult tasks and to accomplish them. While I have withered under the strain at times, others have occasionally benefitted from all my efforts along the way.

My overachieving nature has not made sorting out my calling easy, however. The need to take on something complicated and difficult and to excel at it may have been one of the contributing factors that pushed me to understand my calling to be lifelong, international missionary work. I wanted to do something difficult. I wanted to tackle something that most people were not willing to commit to or try.

There is something like stewardship thrown into this mix as well. My generation has the opportunity and burden of being able to choose from countless options. We can choose whatever will make us happy (as if we know), and for the most part, we have the resources to make anything happen. We are told that if we apply ourselves, we can change the world. Growing up in the church, I heard again and again that we were to offer not just our money but also our time and talents to God. But what did that look like for me, someone already prone to overachieving?

Gifted in math and science at a young age, I thought perhaps I should pursue medicine. After all, medical personnel are especially useful on the missionary field and in times of crisis. Medicine also seemed like a challenge.

In seminary, during breaks from the reoccurring and overwhelming desire never to step foot in a school or to write a paper again, the obligation I internalized to use my gifts to the fullest led me to the thought that maybe I ought to look into PhD programs. Maybe I should research, write, and teach at a university or seminary level. My models of what I might be called to had begun to expand by that time, but I was still trapped by a suffocating layer of responsibility to the mind and abilities I was given.

Later, when I realized how much I loved working with refugees and how successfully I was able to teach in that setting, I wondered if there wasn't some humanitarian crisis out there that I could use my skills to help solve. I'm a great problem solver, and I had always been looking for some problem or some part of the world to devote myself to solving. Maybe that was the hard thing I could do for God. Maybe my calling was tied up in a crisis somewhere.

These *shoulds* and obligations were difficult to get past, but I realized that the problem was much deeper and shadowy. Not long ago, I overheard a woman talking about ministry and achievement. I scribbled down what I heard in my notebook. Afterward, each time I flipped past that page, I groaned.

"Are we using ministry to achieve?" she asked.

We can see how some of the big-name ministers out there manipulate ministry into achievement. We like to look down on their ministry power grabs. Unfortunately, the subtle, unconscious desire to *achieve* something, tackle something, climb some ladder, fix some problem, and get some recognition is a desire I know well. I knew that achievement, while sometimes producing positive results, was actually a heavy lump I was carrying around with me. The need or desire to achieve, even or especially through ministry, is part of my baggage, and the weight of it was interfering with me finding and following my calling.

My need to achieve, even through my calling, has made it difficult to be content to a calling without a title. This baggage makes it hard not to self-identify with what I do and what I can accomplish, especially what I can "accomplish for the kingdom."

I've wondered why I sometimes feel that it's not enough for me to do the work I'm called to—work that is below the surface but still subversive, effective, and important, just without a title or a paycheck to validate it. Sure, there is some injustice in it. In many churches and ministry settings, it is much harder for women to find ways to fulfill their callings that include both a paycheck and a title. I feel this injustice for myself, for the other fabulous women ministers I know, and for the church and world that miss out by not fully embracing these women and their gifts.

However, I've come to the much more uncomfortable hypothesis that my reoccurring dissatisfaction stems not from injustice but from my own unmet need to achieve. That's not a pretty realization. Still, I've learned, and I am learning, that in order to climb mountains and make it through my pilgrimage without the heart and soul's equivalent of a broken back and shin splints, I have to recognize what I am carrying around with me. I have to sort through my baggage and deal with what I find there even when it's heavy or unflattering.

Another piece of baggage that is often heavy and unflattering, but that we all have to sort through, is self-identity.

When I first moved to Denver, I took part in a yearlong, full-time service program. The program was sponsored by AmeriCorps and facilitated by a local faith-based organization. The whole experience was intense and, to be honest, not well executed. The result was something like a year in a pressure cooker.

Eighteen of us had committed to working as full-time volunteers for a year. We also committed to living in "intentional community" in two rundown houses in downtown Denver and to a life of "simplicity." Simplicity meant that we each received a stipend of only $75 per month and a $15 per person weekly grocery budget.

Ten of us lived in one house. We were all young, and we all had self-identity baggage to work through. Many of my housemates were right out of college, but a couple of us were older. One of them was using the year to fulfill an internship requirement after two years in seminary. Our oldest housemate was from Egypt and serving in the United States as a Mennonite service volunteer. I was slightly younger than he was, and I had been out of college for five years and out of seminary for two. I moved to Denver because I saw the program as a way to lean into my calling. The tenets of the program were simplicity, service, spirituality, and hospitality. These tenets were integral to how I was starting to redefine my calling. But I also moved because my husband, David (my boyfriend at the time), lived in Denver, and he had another two years of seminary to go. (And yes, it took some real soul searching and pride checking to make sure I could move across the country to be near a man I loved and not damage my inner feminist.) Third, and finally, I'll be honest: I applied for dozens of jobs with nonprofits and with religious organizations. I applied for jobs for which I had lots of experience and some for which I had no experience. I sent my résumé to places in Texas, and I submitted my résumé for positions in Colorado. I even applied for jobs internationally.

No one was hiring. The other real job option I had at the time—something that paid well, came with benefits, and seemed like a good stepping-stone on my ministry journey—actually offered me a job. Yet they didn't offer me the job until after the most bizarre job interview I've ever had. The interview ended with me crying while the whole panel of interviewers watched. I had finally cracked under the pressure of their bizarre and intensely personal questions, and once I started crying, I couldn't stop. All I could think of was getting out of that room, but in a strange twist of events, those folks seemed to like my tears. They offered me the job. I took a day to think it over before I told them, essentially, *hell no.*

Off to Denver I went. The service program would allow me to be with like-minded people and to get my foot in the door with Denver churches and nonprofit organizations. Or so I thought.

To say that I learned a lot in that year would be an understatement. With all of the people in my house working difficult, emotionally draining jobs in organizations that were often understaffed and unorganized, and all of us living on top of each other in a setting with few creature comforts, no familiar support systems, and no air-conditioning, life grew chaotic. One by one, I watched as my housemates dealt with or avoided self-identity work. That failure led many of them to implode in their jobs and in our community life. It was messy.

Our year was much like climbing a mountain. The stress and intensity of those days meant issues we didn't realize we were carrying around began to weigh heavily on us. Rather than sorting through their expectations, their unmet desires, their past hurts, their uncertainty about who they wanted to be—some of my housemates tried to get acclaim, get noticed, or be liked. Some used situations to feel powerful or to gain control of something, anything, however big or small it might be. (As a result, we had more fights in our community about small things, such as how many bananas to buy each week, than any of us would have imagined possible.)

Some of my housemates continued to operate out of a mode for living that revolved around hiding. Some turned to addiction. And some of us did the best we could to try to achieve and to fix people.

We were in difficult jobs and difficult situations. Those situations revealed the heaviness of the things we were hauling around inside of us. I recognized, especially in the middle of those grueling days, just how much inner work we still had left to do. We had to learn who we were and who we weren't. We had to stand inside our stories, including the parts that we didn't choose or like very much, and learn to let things go. We had to rediscover who we were. I realized that in order to endure the difficult paths of our callings, we would have to know who we were and who we were called be.

All of us have heavy things that will weigh us down if we don't work to dig them out and find resolution. Sometimes things don't start out heavy, but the weight of our unresolved issues begins to dig into our backs over time. Other parts of our past seem like they have been with us since the beginning. We forget that we carry them with us until we are pushed to our limits and feel their true weight and impact. We then realize that our baggage has been influencing the way we have seen God, the world, and our callings all along.

Some of us have to weed through a profound sense of unworthiness. Others have to sort through piles of shame buried deep inside us. For others, it is addictions or pride. Some need to work through what it was like to grow up in a particular family and its surroundings. These things shape all of us, and it's important to know how they have molded us over time and continue to influence us.

Digging through our baggage and letting things go is challenging, messy, internal work. It's understandable to want to continue to carry everything with us. Taking a hard look at what we carry inside us and allowing God to redeem the whole of our lives require us to be vulnerable, but both tasks are important.

I've found it necessary to do the hard internal work so that I can help others. I've learned that until I get my hands dirty in the muck of my own life, dig around, hold it up to God, let it go, and ask for help, I merely end up smearing my muck all over the people around me. My own baggage gets spewed out onto the people I hate, the people I am trying to help, and even the people I love most dearly.

I have gotten the muck of other people's baggage on me over the years, especially when situations get stressful and people get fearful.

We have all watched people do this. People lash out or overreact, and everyone wonders why they are acting that way. So often it results from fear of their own shadowy baggage. It's ugly, and I have done it.

If we want to be able to live into our callings and help instead of hurt people along the way, we have to sort through the baggage we are carrying around with us. The things weighing us down may be different for each one of us. Our baggage might be the way we define success. Can we feel successful without a big, or even just decent, paycheck? Can we feel like we are successful without a title, a spouse, or an audience?

Our baggage might have more to do with feeling inadequate or insecure (or both). It might be anxiety or worry. Maybe it's a crippling fear of failure. Pockets of unforgiveness might weigh us down. The heavy thing in our backpack might be our inability to say no or our feelings of obligation. Maybe we can't get past the notion that we have to live up to the fabled ideal of a good Southern woman or a strong and stoic man. Maybe the pressure is to be an all-knowing academic or a parent who works full-time, fulfills all their parenting duties with flair, and stays fit while doing it.

Baggage comes in all shapes and sizes and weights. We all have it, and on our paths into our callings, as we walk difficult trails and climb mountains, our baggage weighs us down. It tempts us to quit. It clouds our vision. To move forward in our callings, we have to sort through our baggage and leave some of it by the side of the road.

Doing this work means we have to think hard about what we need and what we can live without. Letting go means we won't have everything we want and think we need at all times. Letting go means we will have to admit to God, our community, and ourselves that we don't have our lives put together. But when we are freed of the weight, we can breathe easier, carry ourselves with grace, and even climb mountains.

Chapter 5

Belodorado–Fellow Pilgrims

Walking into Santo Domingo, I had a conversation with a Brazilian man named Ygor. We had interacted here and there throughout my first week on the Camino. He showed up in some of the hostels, I had seen him walking ahead with some other people I'd met, and I'd heard him singing on the trail ahead of me just past Irache, where there is a fountain that dispenses real wine. It's a centuries-long tradition for pilgrims to stop by the vineyard and fill up a cup to cheer them along on their journey.

I happened to pass Irache at about 8:00 in the morning. I put a little wine in an empty extra water bottle, took a sip, and then tucked it away for the evening—or at least the afternoon. Ahead on the trail, I could hear the singing of Ygor and a couple of other Brazilian pilgrims who had all met along the way in the last couple of days. Ygor was obviously taking things as they came—wine included.

Young and over six feet tall, Ygor was a fast walker. So, while we saw each other in the hostels in the evenings, I rarely saw him on the trails during the day. But one day, as both of us were walking into Santo Domingo, we were near each other, and he slowed down to my pace.

"I'm Ygor," he said. "I thought I'd tell you some of my story."

Ygor told me about the divorce he had just been through, the marriage he never imagined would end, his beautiful little girl, the big corporate job from which he had taken a sabbatical, and lessons he was learning on the Camino. There was no small talk with Ygor—only real stories, real problems, real insights.

Nearly all the interactions I had on my pilgrimage were like that. There was something about being on the same journey to Santiago that bonded us, even if we were strangers. Each of us was drawn—called—to the Camino in one way or another, and the stories behind our pilgrimages did not usually involve superficial facts about our lives. The circumstances that pulled us to the Camino often centered on loss or confusion, usually involved searching for meaning or place, and were always, whether we realized it or not, spiritual.

Also driving the conversations and relationships along the Camino was the realization that interactions with fellow pilgrims were often fleeting. Frequently I would see someone only for a short time. Maybe I walked with them during the day or talked with them in the hostels in the evening. Then I might never see them again.

Some people walked faster, and some walked slower. We all had individual rhythms, schedules, and ideals.

I met Thomas and his dad, Peter, both from the Italian-speaking region of Switzerland, in a small hostel in the little town of Belodorado. It had rained all evening, and even with the heat and lights on, the hostel was dark and cold.

We sat around the long wooden table under dim lights, trying to stay warm in the spare clothes we had left as the rest of our clothing tumbled together in the hostel's single dryer. I'd boiled a pot of water and added a large pack of chicken and stars soup mix. The father/son duo had made an elaborate pasta dish, and they insisted I eat some while my pot came to a boil and the pasta stars in my soup mix began to soften. We ate, and when the soup had simmered long enough, I poured everyone at the table a salty bowl.

That night we sat together telling stories long after we had downed the pasta and I'd passed off as much soup as I could. I was fascinated by Thomas and Peter's tales about the coming of age of their relationship. I was intrigued by how they told their stories—the son translating for his dad and adding bits and pieces of commentary on what his father said.

Thomas and Peter no longer lived in the same town; Thomas now had a fancy job in Zurich, Switzerland's capital. They were biking the Camino together both to fulfill lifetime wishes and to spend time together. On bikes, their experience of the Camino was much different than mine. I was staggered to realize how much ground they covered each day. I had been walking for weeks, but they traveled the same distance in mere days on their bicycles.

As we sat around the table talking about our paths, the towns we had passed through, and where we planned to spend the next night, I realized that at such different paces there was zero possibility we would meet again on the Camino. It would not be like the chance reencounters I had with other pilgrims like Ygor, where I would occasionally meet back up with someone I hadn't seen for days.

Unless I took these men up on their offer to be their guest in Switzerland, I would never see them again. I wanted to hear more of their story, and I wanted to hear how their pilgrimage would end. Instead, we savored the moments around that wooden table, shivering in our shorts and warming our insides with salty soup and stories of fellow pilgrims.

The next day, they were off. They left before I woke up, and it's true that I never saw them again.

For a long time, I felt great loss when relationships in my life faded. Growing up, I had worked hard to keep relationships alive from my past and felt guilty when they trailed off. I also felt conflicted when I knew I would be with people for only a short while. Do I invest in that person for a week? For a day or an hour? Will I be able to keep in touch with the person after we part?

As I got older, and especially as I traveled, I developed a new, healthier strategy. I call it my catch-and-release principle. I try to catch people wherever they land in my path. I try to be present for as long as we are together, and then I release them and send them on their diverging path with peace and blessings.

This principle was especially important on my Camino. People came into and out of my path. Sometimes our relationships were single servings, like mine with the bicyclists. Other times I met people and walked almost the entire way to Santiago de Compostela alongside them. The difficult thing in life and on the Camino is that we don't always know who falls into which category. All we can do is receive them all as they come to us and be ready to let them go when they must move on.

By the end of my seminary experience, I had made lots of friends. My school was small, and I quickly got used to the faces that popped up again and again in my classes. On top of that, I was a graduate assistant for the assistant dean of my seminary. People were always coming in and out of his office, and I helped make files for new students, learning their names and faces along the way.

Originally I had a no-nonsense approach to graduate school. I was there to take classes. I was there to learn and prepare. If I made friends along the way, fine, but I didn't need them. I had housemates and friends from undergrad. Besides, I figured that between a full-time course load and multiple jobs, I didn't need social activities to fill the little spare time I had.

I thought I could get by without friends from seminary. I didn't think I would need deep relationships with people who were in the same boat as me. I was wrong. Similar to the people on the Camino, some people in seminary came into my life and hovered in my path for only a semester. Sometimes they were simply a person with whom to share class notes or a classmate whose insightful questions or comments I enjoyed during discussions. Other people and professors stepped in for longer seasons. They gave me company or helped nudge me along my way.

Then there were my girls. I don't know what bonded several of us together so tightly except the fact that we were all struggling along the path of Baptist women who felt called to ministry together. We took turns prodding each other to finish projects. We shared notes and paper-writing strategies. Over class notes or martinis, I listened to the stories of their pasts, and they listened to mine. They brought me dinner when I came to evening classes straight from work. We had coffee dates and ugly-faced cry sessions together.

Mostly, we said some of the most comforting words I've ever heard or given—*Me too*.

My first weeks of college were filled with questions: "Where are you from?" "What's your major?" "What dorm do you live in?" Even when I didn't recognize anyone in a classroom or cafeteria, I knew I had a few crutch questions to get me started. From there I would hope that a common experience or interest would emerge and I would be able to get a conversation rolling.

Much like my first days on a college campus, I discovered a few icebreaker questions to help start conversations with other pilgrims I met on the Camino. (Ygor was an exception. He didn't need an icebreaker to start telling his life story!)

You can start by asking, *Where are you from?* The Camino is a casserole of cultures. I've not come across another place in the world where you can pop into a small-town café, sit with a few strangers, and realize that you have representatives from every continent except Antarctica at the table. I'm a lover of travel and places, and interacting with so many people from so many places on the Camino was exhilarating for me.

The next question is, *Where did you start?* This question is not as practical as the nationality question, but it provides a way to gain context for the person's journey. The second question was the toughest one for me to answer.

I started in Pamplona. It was the most convenient place to begin my journey, even though just getting to Pamplona involved a plane, bus, taxi, second bus, and two-hour walk. I realized that going all the way to Saint Jean Pied de Port, where most international pilgrims begin walking the Camino on the other side of the French border, would have taken me an additional day of buses and trains. Then, once I got to Saint Jean, I would have to turn around and spend three days walking back to Pamplona.

Another option for me had been Roncesvalles. Most Spaniards start walking the Camino on the Spanish side of the border, in a town called Roncesvalles, which is easier than going all the way into France. But for me, getting there would have required too many bus and train rides to make it worth the effort. I figured Pamplona made the most sense. Still, I felt a bit guilty.

Would I be a *real* pilgrim if I started in Pamplona? I finally realized that was a silly question. I planned to hike with my belongings on my back for eight hundred kilometers, around five hundred miles, across an entire country for almost five weeks. Chipping off two or three days from the beginning of my Camino would not make me an illegitimate pilgrim.

I could reconcile the logistics in my mind, but I continued to feel a tinge of regret (or shame?) when for the first few days of my Camino everyone asked where I had started. They had all started at Saint Jean, and I had only just begun in Pamplona. I felt like I had taken the easy route.

Additionally, I would sometimes meet people who had started their pilgrimage to Santiago in Paris or, for one guy, in Amsterdam. What I knew to be an epic undertaking suddenly seem small compared to others' journeys.

Luckily, I had plenty of time to reverse my humbled position. As I walked further toward Santiago, I encountered more and more people who had started even later in the journey than I had. Especially at each major city, I found people just beginning. Rather than feeling a tinge of shame over where I started, I began to feel accomplished and proud of my journey. It's as hard to shake off pride as it is to shake off shame. Either way, it's hard not to compare journeys, even when they are pilgrimages.

The last major influx of pilgrims on the journey comes at the city of Sarria. Sarria is the final major city before the hundred-kilometer mark on the Camino to Santiago. To get official credit with the Catholic Church for making the pilgrimage, pilgrims have to prove, through stamps in their pilgrim passport, that they have walked at least one hundred kilometers of the Camino. Because of this, many people choose to do only the last portion of the Camino, starting in Sarria.

When I arrived in Sarria, the paths of the Camino were noticeably more crowded. People were more cheerful, louder, and less exhausted. (They walked so fast!) I admit that I had to do a bit of interior work to avoid feeling superior to these pilgrims.

And then, on another level entirely, were what the Spanish called *domingueros*. The name comes from the Spanish word *domingo*, which means Sunday. Basically, these "pilgrims" were weekenders. They would pull up to a trailhead and pile out of chartered buses in groups of fifty or sometimes more. They were tourist pilgrims.

I had received the reminder early on in my pilgrim experience that everyone's pilgrimage, everyone's Camino, is different. I tried to take that sentiment to heart. It was true, and I knew it. My experience was different from that of everyone with whom I talked, at least on some level. Some started their journey before me, some after. Some people were younger or more athletic than I was, while others were older or wheezed their way up the hills.

Some people traveled faster, some even on bicycles. Other people walked only ten kilometers a day. I had given myself forty days to get to Santiago, while these slower walkers would need to walk about eighty days to make it to the end of the journey.

Even though I knew those differences existed, it was hard not to be grumpy when a group of *domingueros* flooded the trail for the day, looking at me curiously as I shuffled along. It was also hard not to feel a bit of pride when I met someone whose journey on foot would be only half as long as mine. And, at the same time, I also had trouble not feeling somewhat inferior for starting my journey two or three days in.

Wrapped up in this is an innate temptation to compare ourselves to others. The same thing happens when it comes to calling. We all know it's stifling to compare ourselves to other people, but it's hard not to. How has he been able to start his own nonprofit? Seriously, *him?* And why is she in a ministry position with a title, a paycheck, and benefits, and I'm just an office manager? Why is he asked to preach and I'm not? I can look around and feel like I am not getting a fair shake compared to others.

Of course, this works in the opposite direction as well. It's ugly to admit, but we all know we are better off than that person over there who will never get to the place to which she thinks she is called. And we look at people just starting and say, "Buckle up, buster—it's a long ride, and you are just beginning." We want to compare blisters and scars and come up on top. We want to compare schedules or speaking engagements and come out busier and therefore more important. We want to compare titles or credentials or connections or schisms that we have endured.

There are lots of ways to compare journeys. We know, if even only on a subconscious level, which tactics will make us feel good about where we are and which ones will make us feel sorry for ourselves and our lot in life.

Comparing ourselves to others is a terrible practice. The lenses we use to compare aren't fair to ourselves or to them. Additionally, looking at life and other people through these lenses is not usually realistic. What lies under the surface of social media, scholarship award lists, or denominational titles is often not what it seems. People are always more complex than we give them credit for. Unfortunately, we miss what people around us can offer when we are too preoccupied with figuring out whose journey has been harder and more deserving of respect.

What I realized on the Camino, and what has proven true in situations since, is that we all have a subtle and deep-seated fear of *not enough*. There don't seem to be enough jobs for all of us. There's not enough respect to go around. There aren't enough mentors, and there aren't enough spouses. There aren't enough paychecks, and there aren't enough people to realize how hard we have worked.

When our hearts or our experiences tell us that there's *not enough* out there in the world, we start to compare. When we look around and realize what we *don't* have, we start to think that *we are not enough.* We start to believe that others around us *aren't enough.* It's a terrible cycle, but it's the natural progression.

Comparison leads to superiority or insecurity or, more often, to both. Either way, comparing ourselves to others—comparing the city we started our hike in, our résumés, our status, our blisters, or how fast we walk without stopping—leads to isolation. When we think we aren't good enough, or if we think that we are imposters—to be found out at any minute!—then we aren't likely to let people get close. They might see us as the frauds we think we are.

If we think that others have one-dimensional stories of undeserved success, or if we think they are not thriving precisely because they don't deserve to, we won't get close enough to them to let the illusion wear off. We won't test the illusion for the fear that we will find out that she looks just like us and that his failures and successes are just like ours—or just like our best friend's, our brother's, or our mother's.

Comparison dooms us. It dulls us. Theodore Roosevelt said that comparison is the thief of joy. Comparison cuts us off from the very people we need in our life—the people who say that if we pool our resources, there's enough for all of us.

I spent almost an entire morning on the Camino walking with Karl from Austria. I had been startled to find him ahead of me on the path that morning, singing a bit to himself. He was the first person I had seen since taking the more scenic, shaded, and less used branch of the Camino that morning. Karl, a fast walker, was used to hiking alone, but we hiked through the trees and up the hillside together for a while. To keep up, I walked quickly and asked questions so that he could do the talking while I did the deep breathing.

We talked, of course, about where we were from (Austria and Texas), where we had started our Caminos (Saint Jean and Pamplona), and why we were walking the Camino. Karl told me that he was struggling to find meaning and direction—a common theme for many on the Camino.

Before long, the Camino flattened out and the branch Karl and I had taken met back up with the other branch. In the flat distance, we saw a familiar backpack. *Red backpack . . . red backpack . . . Michel!* We were getting good at recognizing pilgrims by their clothing and gear (much easier to do when it's the same clothing and gear day after day!). A bit ahead of him, we saw gray shorts and quickly identified Roberto. Near him was Steve in his floppy brown hat.

There was no escaping the heat that day. The sun blared down on us, and after the trail flattened out, all the trees disappeared. I wouldn't be able to keep up my pace with Karl much longer. Finally, our group happened upon one lonely tree. It wasn't a big tree, and it had only patchy beginnings of leaves and flowers. Sitting close enough to smell each other, though, we all fit under the tree's shade.

Break time rituals commenced. We threw down backpacks and pulled off hiking boots with a sigh. We unpacked water bottles first and took long sips. We splashed a tiny bit on our faces and then began to dig out snacks.

What I remember most about this afternoon was that it reminded me of the feeding of the five thousand. Granted, we were only five, but it felt like a miracle nonetheless. It was well into the afternoon, and none of us had eaten lunch on that uninhabited stretch of path.

Hot and huddled under the tree, we were an eclectic mix of French, Italian, Austrian, American, and German. We didn't understand much of what the others were saying, but we did understand what was happening. My apricots were passed around. With a smile, Roberto said that if I didn't eat some of his cookies, he would *break my face.* The night before, I had told Roberto that *ti spacco la faccia* is the only Italian phrase I know, so I assumed he was joking with me. Just in case, I ate some anyway.

Soon we were all sharing. We had an assortment of cereal bars, cookies, nuts, and fruit to fill us all. We couldn't say much, but I'd like to think that we all understood that in sitting in the same shade, sharing what little food we carried on our backs, something simple, joyful, and profound was happening.

The truth I learned that day is that there's enough to go around. You, even if you don't speak my language, even if you are not like me, are enough. You have something to contribute—even, or especially, if it's a bag of peanuts. When we get close enough to realize that we all sweat, that we all need some shade and rest, and that we are all on the same journey no matter how or where we started or how long we will walk together, we realize that we are each enough. It's a freeing and nourishing realization.

I've also come to understand that if I don't take the time to sit under the trees and around the wooden tables of life, I will miss out on all kinds of people who could have been meaningful in my journey.

What good is it to speak to a father on a bicycle whom I will never see again? Well, I'm still talking about our conversation years later.

Whether people are part of our journey for a season or a day or a lifetime, it's important to open our arms to them. The journey of discovering and living out our callings will require support, reminders that we are not alone, and, occasionally, a good old uncomfortable lesson learned.

We can't walk this journey of calling alone. We need people to carry extra snacks. We need people to start conversations that we don't yet know how to start. We need people to say *me too* and *it's okay* and *here is my story*. We need seasoned pilgrims to give us perspective.

These fellow pilgrims might be right in front of us, or we may have to look for them. They can be mentors, colleagues, siblings, or neighbors. They might be our postal carrier, our classmates, a pastor across town, or our archenemy. The pilgrims that are meant to walk with us for a time might be outside our tradition. They might be outside our socioeconomic status, our gender, or our ethnicity. They might be rough around the edges at first glance. They may have had journeys that seem longer and more difficult than ours or journeys that seem shorter and easier than ours.

Look around. Reach out. Get close enough to others that the lenses we use to compare ourselves to others no longer work.

Calling is a hard journey, but one of the best parts is that we can't, and don't have to, do it alone.

Chapter 6

Burgos—We All Need Rest

The day I walked into Burgos was long and unglamorous. I had stopped for the previous night in San Juan de Ortega at an old cloistered monastery. Many pilgrims walk all the way to Ages, a bigger town that would make for a shorter hike into Burgos the next day. But by the time I got to San Juan de Ortega, I was ready for a break.

There wasn't much to San Juan de Ortega, only a small Romanesque church with a half-ruined cloister-turned-pilgrim-hostel standing next to it. All that was left of the town square was an old stone fountain, a drink machine, and a bar/café that had closed just before I showed up and didn't reopen again for a very hungry three and a half hours.

I checked into the monastery-turned-pilgrim-hostel and took a shower. As I did every day, I hand washed my laundry. I was instructed to let my clothes dry on the pillars of the thousand-year-old courtyard. I complied, but not without a sense of guilt for disrespecting the historic building. I walked through the ruins of the other half of the monastery and went to the church next door. I took a quick tour of the dark church, said a prayer, and then, with the rest of the pilgrims who had missed the kitchen cut-off at the café, sat in the sun outside like a hungry dog, waiting for it to reopen.

My tired legs and the fascinating monastery ruins weren't the only reasons I stopped in San Juan de Ortega. I knew most of the pilgrims who were staying there that night. Almost all of us had started the day in Belodorado, and most of us had been at the same hostel the night before. Some people walk faster and some walk slower, but many of us had been walking at the same pace for a good portion of the Camino.

Truth be told, I had become quite attached to many of these pilgrims. Seeing their faces along the paths, in the hostels, and around the towns in the evenings made me feel as if I were a part of a special community. We shared stories about our lives and about our blisters. The people I was meeting were becoming the most joyful and poignant part of my Camino experience. The main reason I stopped in San Juan was that I didn't have much more time with many of these pilgrims.

Burgos is one of the biggest cities along the Camino. It represents the end of roughly the first third of the Camino de Santiago for those who started near the Spanish border. Some pilgrims trek right through the city of Burgos without veering off the yellow-arrowed path, but most pilgrims spend at least one night in Burgos and see a bit of the city. Often pilgrims stay two nights, using one night to recover from the day's hike and then a whole day to see Burgos and recharge on a bit of city life.

Others leave the Camino altogether once they get to Burgos. Some go back home and return later to complete an additional third or another week's worth at another time. Others, short on time, take a bus or train from Burgos to other cities further along the Camino, speeding up their journey. In my case, I left the Camino from Burgos for a short weekend trip to visit friends on Spain's northern coast.

Burgos was a meeting and scattering point along the journey. I was always meeting people and never knowing whether I would see them again. This adding in or dropping off had happened all along the way for the first third of my Camino, but Burgos would be the first real scattering for me. I would miss these pilgrims whose faces and stories had become familiar. I realized that once I returned from my weekend in the north, I wouldn't know anyone on the Camino.

Though I was excited to see familiar faces in the north, where I had lived and taught English for a year during college, I was surprised at how attached I had become to my fellow Camino pilgrims. So when most of the people I knew on the trail said they were staying in San Juan for the night, I stopped and stayed too. I figured that an extra night with people I had come to love and whom I would likely never see again would make the next day's long hike worth it.

The hike from San Juan de Ortega into Burgos was indeed a long one. It was also trying. A bit of a map with some vague instructions for an alternate path into Burgos was taped to the door of the pilgrim's hostel in San Juan. I had noticed it that morning as I left the hostel, a bit later than most pilgrims like usual, but I didn't make much out of it. I didn't like veering off the official path and risking getting lost.

It didn't take me long to do exactly that, though. I got lost. There were several places along the way where the arrows were conflicting. What I didn't realize at the time is that residents in a few crafty small villages put up their own arrows to trick people into looping through their towns and cafés. I came to one place that had signs marking the road ahead as both the right *and* wrong way. Needless to say, I walked loops inside that tiny town for a while before I found my way out and back to the main path.

Not even calculating my village wanderings, I ended up taking the longest way possible to Burgos. I hiked thirty-five kilometers, more than twenty-one miles, on terrain that alternated between steep, rock-strewn hills and bleak, tarry, industrial wastelands. Spoiled by the dozens of small medieval towns and sweeping landscapes filled with vineyards that I had encountered again and again thus far in my Camino, I was taken aback by the blunt return to the ugly edges of modern civilization.

The hike into Burgos was also the point on the Camino where everything below my shins began to unravel. I played basketball all through middle school and high school, even though my body was distinctly not made for it. I came to love sports, but no one ever called me athletic. I could hustle. I learned plays and studied game film. Still, I remained one of the clumsiest and least naturally inclined players my coaches had ever seen. I ended games with ice packs, sometimes three or more, and ended high school with an ankle that popped after every other step.

In my regular life, my ankle didn't bother me too much anymore. I'd given up basketball years ago, and despite the fact that my ankle would sometimes pop loudly as I walked through quiet libraries, I never gave it much thought.

For most of my first few days on the Camino, IcyHot and ibuprofen did the trick. There was some pain in my ankles, but it was manageable. After a few more days, it came time for me to strap on my trusty ankle brace. Eventually, by the time I wandered through the entirety of Burgos's outlying industrial parks, navigating steep downhill passages strewn with golf ball-sized rocks and getting lost in the outlying villages all in the same day, my ankle pain became excruciating. I resorted to the only thing that alleviated the pain a little: limping.

Limping was a shortsighted strategy, and I knew it. Limping leads to the thing you want to avoid most on the Camino de Santiago (outside of bedbugs). The bane of all pilgrims is blisters. Blisters are game changers. Blisters are the reason, in the middle of a twenty-one-mile hike with all my luggage on my back, I sat down right in the middle of the sidewalk of a confusing little village. I pulled off my boots and pulled out the safety pin, needle, thread, and hand sanitizer that I carried just for this purpose.

In the middle of the sidewalk, I gave myself impromptu blister surgery.

The Camino de Santiago is many things. One thing the Camino de Santiago certainly is *not* is glamorous.

Overall, the day I hiked into Burgos was hot and confusing. After finally making it through the industrial area and into the city, I also got lost trying to find the city center and the main pilgrim hostel. I only found it when I did because I ran across a pilgrim friend who had made it into town much earlier. He must have recognized my frazzled state because he turned around and personally escorted me to the hostel.

Making it to the hostel in Burgos meant I could prop up my feet and take a much-needed break. While I needed a break, I was surprised at how hard it was to think about taking a couple of days off the Camino, even to go see friends and former colleagues.

I hadn't seen these people for a couple of years. They had been the lifeblood of my first real time away from everything that was familiar to me. That weekend, I would even be able to go to a Sunday service at the tiny church I had been a part of during my year there, meaning I would get to see even more friends. I wanted to see them. The long-distance bus routes that went to the city I used to live in conveniently ran right through Burgos. It was only a few hours away, due north. It made sense to take the trip to see them once I made it to Burgos.

But I was not ready to stop. I wasn't ready for a weekend away from the Camino. The strange thing was that I wasn't even sure how I felt about the day off I had planned just to see the city of Burgos before taking my weekend trip. I was about one-third of the way through the Camino, and I had yet to take a rest day. As funny as it seemed just a couple of weeks into the experience, I no longer remembered what a day away from the Camino—its rhythms, people, and smells—felt like.

Besides, what would I do during that time off? Would I be able to return to the Camino afterwards without sacrificing the physical, emotional, or spiritual progress I had made as a pilgrim? Did I deserve a break? Was that cheating?

The rhythm of the Camino and its people, especially the ones who would continue to walk forward from Burgos, pulled me along. Painfully and thankfully, as has often been the case in my life, even though I didn't know how to stop, my body and my schedule called out for rest. I had no choice. If I was going to see friends, it had to happen while I was at Burgos. If I was going to be able to walk to Santiago, or ever after, I had to rest.

During the Camino and since, I have had to come to terms with the fact that I am not good at resting. I'm not good at taking breaks. I'm good at achieving, and for most of my life, I have leaned into that achievement. Often I leaned into that achievement without realizing what I was sacrificing to get something done.

I have been blessed with lots of ability, and I have spent a large portion of my life figuring out how to push that ability into yet another gear. When I'm not achieving, or don't at least have something productive to show for my time and myself, I start to feel guilty.

I haven't learned rest or balance easily. I never recognized Sabbath commandments as real or important commandments for contemporary living, and I didn't make the discovery logically or painlessly.

Unfortunately, I've only learned to prioritize rest the hard way. I have come to realize that unless I take breaks, I start limping.

I can push onward for a while. It's true. But all that does is create and compound problems. Blisters don't care how good your intentions are. When there is friction on your skin for long enough, you will get a blister. Likewise, when we limp along through life, pushing ourselves and prioritizing our ministries, our callings, or our careers without rest, problems start piling up.

Relationships splinter. Bodies break down. Souls get weary.

Despite how easily I forget it, we need rest. We need breaks. Taking regular breaks is so important that the instruction to do so made it into the Ten Commandments. Resting is a commandment, and an important one, but it's also a gift. Sabbath in the Bible is about resting and feasting. It is about leaning into relationships—with God and with our community.

Sabbath is a celebration, but it is also about the miracle of being made whole. Sabbath provides the space for healing—for stretching out withered hands, for straightening backs that have been bent, and for reminding us that we are more than our accomplishments.

I wish I were better at Sabbath on a small and large scale. I wish that I were born with a stronger ability to regulate myself and my energy. I wish that I were better at resting. Instead of opening my arms to these life lessons, I charge onward, and instead of accepting limits, I end up in the equivalent of being down on the ground in the middle of a small Spanish village performing crude and unglamorous blister surgery.

We can't constantly go without rest and not have problems. I've tried. God made us as humans, and humans need rest—for our bodies and for our souls.

I finally made it to the big pilgrim's hostel in Burgos. Many of the pilgrims I'd met in the first third of my Camino were there. Since lots of people spend an extra night in Burgos, I was able to see some of the people who had gotten a day or two ahead of me on the trail, too.

After showering, doing the daily laundry, and enjoying a celebratory dinner of *doner kebabs* (deliciously greasy Turkish fast food), several of us went to the special pilgrim's Mass at one of the most beautiful cathedrals in all of Europe. Afterwards we met up for wine and *tapas* with other pilgrim friends, staying up well past our normal pilgrim bedtime of about 8:45 p.m. Our group represented six continents, and over glasses of *tinto* and *calimocho,* we celebrated together—celebrated making it that far and celebrated our much-deserved break.

Several of us took the next day off. My time in Burgos was one of the highlights of my entire Camino. In what felt like playing hooky from school, I met up with Ygor and another Brazilian friend for a breakfast of *churros y chocolate* at one of the local cafés. As we sat in a row on the bar stools at the counter, we all reveled in the joy of the moment—fried dough, a day without carrying our packs, a beautiful city. An upbeat song came on the stereo, and before I knew it, the three of us were dancing and spinning around on our stools.

I marveled at the inside of the cathedral after breakfast, bumping into my long-lost and very first pilgrim friend, Claire. I hadn't seen her in weeks. Among some of the most celebrated art in Spain, we caught up on our time apart, our journeys, and how they had diverged. Claire had arrived in Burgos the day before and was headed back out to the trail after her tour of the cathedral.

At the entrance to the cathedral, I wished her a *buen Camino* and gave her a hug. She picked up her walking stick and continued on her way to Santiago.

From there, I made my way along the riverbank to a monastery. Pilgrim friends tipped me off that there was an inhabited and cloistered monastery a couple of kilometers from the city that allowed people to tour its thousand-year-old grounds. The monastery felt like a time machine. I walked in the grooves worn into its original wooden floor and marveled at robes kings wore centuries ago.

Afterwards, I had coffee with Juanma and Maica, a retired couple from Seville to whom I had grown close. They were heading out the next day, while I would be traveling to the northern coast. We shared a *café con leche* together, and then I took in a sight that was even more beautiful than the inside of the cathedral—a fully stocked pharmacy. I restocked my supply of ibuprofen and purchased blister bandages of all shapes and sizes. My Sevillian friends had given me a pilgrim's vocabulary lesson, and I was finally able to get the pharmacist to help me restock my *es-para-dra-po*, or athletic tape.

On the way back to the hostel for the night, I passed a small church preparing for a concert to inaugurate holy week. I stepped inside and decided to stay. The chapel was filled to capacity, something I had rarely seen in Spain at that point. The rustling of bodies and bags soon settled as the choir began to sing. The harmonies bounced around that old church and filled what felt like every square inch of the chapel.

I closed my eyes and let my spirit settle into the music. I felt my body and my spirit sigh. I realized I'd been using up my reserves and pushing my limits on the Camino. It's good to stretch ourselves, but there is a point where stretching begins to hurt rather than help. I was doing just that, returning to an old habit of pushing too far.

When I found myself completely depleted after seminary, I asked myself what I had done that I was so worn out. Why was my seminary experience so draining? The exhaustion wasn't from the depth of study or the hundreds of papers I wrote. My fatigue was largely from the pace I adopted. My fatigue was the pressure to excel—the pressure I had always put on myself, the pressure I felt as a woman in a setting that was largely populated by men, and the pressure to do justice to my gifts.

Throughout seminary I took full loads, worked three part-time jobs, and got A's in every single class except for my last one. Instead of consistent, full nights of rest, I perfected the "caffeine power nap" (a technique that is good for paper writing but bad for your soul). I graduated essentially a year and a half before I had planned. I was finished, and I was out of breath. I hadn't come up for air for two and a half years.

I remember a question a theology professor posed during a lecture on the Trinity. He asked, "What if who we really are only exists in our relationships?" I remember thinking at the time that I was in trouble if that were the case. Pushing myself to the brink, I barely saw the people I lived with, let alone any other friends. "Who I was" started wearing thin.

I was limping along, blistering myself inside and out.

In the days before my sabbatical and my Camino, I'm not sure I would have been able to stop for those few rest days in Burgos and beyond. I don't know if I would have had *churros*, twirling on bar stools with Brazilians, or taken the weekend to see old friends and the coast. I don't know if I would have been able to stop.

Without stopping, I would've missed so much. Without stopping, I don't know if I would have made it to the end of my journey in Santiago.

The fact of the matter is that growing into and walking out our callings is hard, strenuous work. There are rocky hills, and there are small villages setting out confusing signs to trip us up. Sometimes the industrial parks and asphalt-covered airports will convince us that there is nothing beautiful left to be seen in this world.

We are led to believe that we will let people down if we stop to rest, but most often the opposite is true. Not resting usually means that we miss the chance to make memories and strengthen relationships. It also usually means that further along in our journey, we will find ourselves in pain, with blistered relationships or overwhelmed souls. It's nearly impossible to be present to the people and places around us over the noise of our own aches.

We need to rest. We need to let our lives refill with the joy that comes from relationships with God and our community. We need to resist the pull to keep marching forward. Our only other choice is to miss out, burn out, and compound problems.

Sometimes we need rest in the form of beauty and bandages, and other times we need *churros* and chapels and dancing to cheesy pop music. However it comes, our hearts, our minds, and our ankles need a rhythm of rest, and an important part of our walk into our calling is learning how to stop and hear it.

Chapter 7

The Meseta—Ditching the Constraints

The *meseta*, the flat portion of the Camino de Santiago that begins after Burgos, wasn't so bad at first. It is somewhat famed for being boring and flat. Some pilgrims who are crunched for time will walk to Burgos, take a bus to León (the next major city, which is located more or less where the meseta ends), and resume their pilgrimage there. For people who feel the need to leave out a section of their Camino, skipping the meseta seems like the obvious answer.

With so much buildup for the meseta, I walked through the outskirts of Burgos preparing myself to begin what I imagined would be my long and boring journey through the barren Spanish flatlands. I was bolstered by a couple days of rest, and I figured I would need it.

I'll admit that at first I was surprised at how much I liked the regions that made up the Spanish meseta. I wondered if during the years I lived in west Texas I had cultivated a special affinity for flat, open spaces. The flatness of the land seemed to give me more space for breathing. I've often felt claustrophobic after spending time in cities filled with skyscrapers. Vast expanses of land offer me space and speak to me in a language unlike any other landscape.

The meseta also seemed so much greener than I had imagined it would be. Often people spoke of it as a scorched plain, dry and depressingly beige. To my surprise, the path through the meseta was more often a dirt path through a vast, green barley field. The blue skies, red dirt, and green grass stretched forward for miles each day like a painting done in contrasting colors.

The land was flat, and the hiking was relatively easy. Occasionally I would happen across a tall hill to climb, but aside from those rare moments, I just walked forward, straight into the horizon. I got used to hearing the steady rhythm of my steps and my walking stick. The sound provided momentum, a kind of metronome, which propelled me forward.

The other main complaint made about the meseta is that it's boring. There is some truth to that claim. Along with a relatively unchangingly flat landscape, the area the Camino covers in the meseta is not nearly as full of enchanting towns bursting with charming cafés as other sections of the pilgrimage. The towns are quite spread apart and often aren't much more than medieval-style Spanish ghost towns.

Hiking through this part of the country, it became necessary to pack a lunch in case I didn't come across a place to eat during the day. It was during my walk through the meseta that this city girl finally broke her fear of peeing outside. Fortunately, fellow travelers had become sparse. Unfortunately, so had the trees.

The meseta portion of the Camino is boring for some. After all, it *is* flat. It *is* less populated. The landscape *is* monotonous. Yet the reality for me was that my pilgrimage through the meseta was anything but boring.

One thing that takes a while to sink in about this kind of long-distance hiking is that the journey is not a day trip. The journey is not short, and it's not flexible. A pilgrimage does not get rescheduled due to a bit of bad weather. Pilgrimages do not get rescheduled even for a *lot* of bad weather.

Bad weather, it turns out, is exactly what I had while I walked through the meseta.

I had chosen late spring as the best time for me to walk the Camino. I had heard that summertime pilgrimages were often met with relatively large crowds in the hostels, sometimes with pilgrims turned away because all the beds were full. The Spanish heat, even in the northern parts of the country, can be brutal, requiring pilgrims to carry extra reserves of water. During the summer, some pilgrims wake early in the morning, well before dawn, just to beat the heat and the crowds. None of that interested me.

I also knew that Spain can conversely be quite cold, especially in the mountainous west where the Camino ends. Winter was out, but I didn't want to get too far into its shoulder seasons either. Some pilgrims have talked about getting caught in snowstorms as late as April and as early as October in Galicia on the western coast.

Looking for the best weather and the most comfortable number of fellow pilgrims on the trail, as well as determining what fit best into my sabbatical outline and the amount of days remaining on my tourist visa, I decided to walk the Camino in late spring. I figured that the days wouldn't be too hot or too cold, and I imagined walking through fields of wildflowers and budding crops. I bought a cheap rain jacket before I left but didn't think too much of the weather.

Up until my time on the meseta, the weather had been relatively warm. Everyone was complaining about the high temperatures, but as a Texan, I was enjoying the 80s and low 90s. There were some hot days, but it simply meant that when I hand washed my hiking clothes in the late afternoons, they would dry on the clothesline (or a monastery's ancient stone column) in less than an hour.

As soon as I walked out of Burgos, the weather changed. It was holy week, and according to the TVs playing the news in cafés or a glance at the horizon, a system of thunderstorms would take over almost all of Europe until after Easter.

At the beginning of the week, the mornings were clear. I got in some good miles before stopping for a midday snack. But whenever I found a nice boulder or bench to sit on and unpack my sandwich along the path, the clouds began to look unsettling.

The green of the fields stretching into the horizon seemed to intensify. The clouds grew darker and closer as electricity began to fill the air. Hours later, leaving puddles instead of footsteps, I would arrive at my hostel for the night just as the storms were finishing.

Other days the storms clapped and thrashed on through the night. The next morning, the socks I had placed near the radiators were still wet, and my boots sat by the front door of the hostel just as muddy and soaked as I had left them the day before. Chilled from damp clothes and with little other choice, each morning I packed up, put on my cheap and not-so-waterproof jacket, and got moving to warm up.

If the rainstorms had happened a week earlier or maybe a week later, before or after my trek through the meseta, I might have been able to duck out of the worst of the storms by drinking extra *café con leche* in the little bars/cafés that dotted the towns along most of the Camino's path. I could usually follow the yellow arrows right into dark Spanish bars where a smoke-creased grandfather would alternate reading the paper with pouring coffee after coffee until it was time to turn on a soccer game and pour beer after beer. Normally, I didn't have to look for warm cafés. Usually they found me as soon as I entered towns or right before I left the town's edge, with plenty more cafés sandwiched in the town's center.

In the Camino's meseta, though, where towns are spread further apart, I was typically out of luck. If it rained, I got wet. There was no coffee or café to warm me up.

One morning I was walking along with wet boots, wet socks, wet pants, and a wet shirt under my "waterproof jacket." I had a plastic cover to keep my backpack dry, but at that point I was pretty sure that everything inside my backpack not packaged away in plastic shopping bags was wet too. It had rained all morning.

Just when I was getting annoyed by the water already starting to wrinkle my skin, the rain changed. It started hitting me a bit more forcefully. I did not register immediately what was happening, but within fifteen seconds the ground I was walking on was covered in white hailstones.

Instinctively I gathered up my tired and soaked bones and started to make a run for it. I ran a few feet, and then I looked around. Where did I think I was running, anyway? There was nothing but horizon around me. There wasn't a town for miles. There weren't even any buildings or trees in the foreseeable distance.

I stopped my jog. I sloshed on at a slightly faster pace than before, but I didn't run. I just put one foot in front of the other, squishing water out of my boots with each step. When the hail started to smart as it pelted me in the head, I held up the hood of my jacket a few inches from my scalp to keep their impact from thumping me repeatedly. And I kept walking.

Even at the time, I was sure that over the centuries many pilgrims have had the same, or worse, weather conditions. I was sure that my experience would bond me to the millions of pilgrims who had walked the open spaces of the meseta before me.

The water that didn't dry up started to get to me. The paths were wet, and I sloshed through mud all day long. My clothes didn't dry overnight. Sometimes I didn't even bother washing them since they got a good soaking during the day. If there wasn't a dryer in the hostel, I knew I would be putting on cold, damp clothes in the morning. I had two pairs of socks, so I could usually manage to start the day with dry socks, although the dryness never lasted long.

My hiking boots, on the other hand, would not dry. I had received what seemed like good advice not to get waterproof hiking boots. I was told that if the boots were sealed too well, my feet would bake inside them in the typical heat. That made sense to me. I went to my local outdoor outfitter in Texas before I left and found heavy-duty hiking shoes that would be supportive and let my feet breathe.

I bought the boots and tried to break them in for what little time I had before I started my Camino. The soles felt solid, but the shoes weren't too heavy. They seemed like a good fit. On the meseta, though, even without heavy leather or excessive padding, when the boots got wet they were hard to get dry.

All that moisture was also seeping into my skin. I would take off my shoes and socks at the end of the day to find wrinkled masses attached to my ankles. Even worse, I started to get new blisters. The calluses I had built up by that point, which had largely protected me until then, were waterlogged. Each day I had new blisters. Each day I had more pain.

After a week of wet pain, I got ready to start the day's hike and found my hiking boots still wet by the hostel door. I decided not to put them on. In what felt mostly like giving up, I ditched my hiking boots for the day and walked in sandals instead.

I'd carried along a pair of sandals with me the whole way. I used them to walk around town in the evening so that my feet could breathe and relax after a day in hiking boots. I used the sandals when I showered to protect my feet from the feet of all those other pilgrims. Slipping into them at the end of the day was luxurious, relaxing, and freeing.

I decided to wear them on the trail. I'll be honest: it mostly seemed that hiking in sandals couldn't actually be worse than hiking in blistering, wet boots for another consecutive day.

I was taken aback by the stir my sandals caused, though. Any time I passed someone, a pilgrim or a Spaniard, they commented on my footwear. *Hiking in sandals! In the rain no less!* I got in the habit of telling people I had figured out the secret to keeping my socks dry— by not wearing any. My feet, it turned out, were much more waterproof than my hiking boots.

My toes got a little cold at times, but that was about the extent of my problems with this new philosophy on footgear. And, with the pain I frequently felt in my feet, going a little numb wasn't much of a drawback. My feet and sandals would get covered in mud, but then I could just walk through the next puddle and wash everything off. No wet socks chafed my feet. I didn't have to worry about socks or boots drying out by the next morning.

Sandals turned out to be an ideal solution to wet footgear.

What I soon realized was that I would have been better off in my sandals all along. I was wearing my boots because that was what I was supposed to do. I was given good advice about hiking shoe choices. My choices were logical and fit well within the standard pilgrim guide-lines. Yet, in the end, those shoes didn't fit my needs.

I didn't realize until I switched over to mostly wearing my sandals, especially in the rain, that the hiking shoes had constrained me. They had given me blisters. The shoes were subtly suffocating me.

As I walked along in sandals, I was confusing some people, but my feet felt great. I had to explain to every third person why I was wearing sandals and that, yes, they were supportive enough and, no, I wasn't doing terrible damage to my feet. I still slipped into my hiking boots when they were dry to give my feet a change of pace, but only for a bit here and there. The barefoot girl I have always been got a chance to resurface and let her feet feel the sunshine (and the rain).

As I carried on, walking into the horizon all day, I spent a lot of time thinking about those sandals. The unchanging landscape of the meseta left me plenty of time to turn inward and observe my changing inner landscape instead. I wished that I had ditched the hiking boots sooner. I realized some of the damage I had done to myself was due to being unwilling or unable to change my footwear.

I also realized that my boots were a metaphor. Like my boots, I had been walking inside some other models throughout my life that, looking back, didn't fit me well.

I found that it was relatively easy for me to think that I was blazing new trails throughout my life. I did do things that my peers weren't doing and took risks that others didn't take. My path certainly looked different than the paths of others. My journey was different, but my journey was also shaped by a host of influences. It took a long time and a lot of discomfort for me to realize the way these influences were shaping me.

What I finally discovered was that I had subscribed to a whole host of ways of living and following my calling that I simply inherited or absorbed. I didn't even know that there were other choices, other models, or other ways of walking forward.

I took some of the models I was given for granted. It wasn't until my mind, my emotions, my creativity, and my soul were soggy and blistered that I realized I had been trying to live into my calling in ways that didn't *fit*. I was slow to realize that life, especially the life of ministry and calling, doesn't have to follow the limited patterns we have seen. I do not have to try to squeeze myself into life's version of wet hiking boots.

The models of calling so many of us have absorbed or inherited tend to be limited. These are also so well integrated into our thinking that we often don't realize we are using them. I thought that the way I had learned to think about calling was how calling was. I didn't know there were options.

I didn't know that gender did not define calling. I didn't know that calling wasn't synonymous with career. I didn't know that calling could encompass all my life and not just the parts that I had seen labeled as "ministry" before. I didn't know calling could mean something other than being on staff at a church or on the mission field. I didn't know that once I surrendered to a calling, life wouldn't just take care of itself from there.

I didn't know that there was more to it than a one-size-fits-all approach.

I've tried on and walked a few miles in lots of different ways to think about calling and ministry. Some ways were helpful, and some ways felt foreign. I have clumsily stomped around in some ill-fitting models as well. They weren't very helpful, but they did give me the freedom to experiment. Trying on new ways to think about calling helped me to develop my imagination. It helped me realize that there are other ways of thinking about my path in life.

I have landed on a model of thinking about ministry and calling that I think is truly helpful. For me, it is a shoe that fits—it lets me breathe, it supports me, and it also gives me the freedom to be the barefooted girl I have always been. Thinking about calling this way changed the game for me. The pain of blisters and chafing eased.

For me, the most helpful model has been to think about calling as the *theme* of my life. For a person like myself who loves concrete ways to think about things—who likes to hold things in her hand and turn them and poke them—*theme* might seem a surprising choice. Yet this model took deep root in me and helped me began to make sense of so much of my experience. Now, I speak of my calling primarily through the lens of *theme*.

Themes in general, whether in literature, film, or art, are about context and patterns. Themes are the strings woven throughout a story, a film, a painting, or a life.

Themes are can be subtle. Sometimes they hover just below the surface. To find themes, we have to take a close look at the underlying motives and the less obvious stories in each episode and also zoom out and have a look through a wide-angle lens. Like art, we need to see the full exhibit to spot the recurring motifs.

When I stumbled upon this model, I began to ask myself what the patterns of my life were. What was my theme? I looked at the big picture. I took in the arc of my life. I'll be honest. At first glance, it was difficult to find any kind of cohesive thread.

I then started examining my life's random collections of episodes, beginning with the jobs and experiences that made me feel like I was alive with purpose. I wasn't sure at first what they had in common. How could I string together jobs such as teaching English and American culture to middle school students in Spain and to African refugees in west Texas with jobs like working with the homeless in downtown Denver and editing ethics books?

Eventually I began to see a pattern emerge. These jobs had something in common with my love for gathering friends and strangers around my table. The thing they had in common explained the amount of time I spend texting, having coffee with, and listening to friends. I realized that the thing I really loved, the thing I was really good at, is walking alongside people. I have often found that the people who cross my paths are in transition. Sometimes that transition was a big one, like transitioning from a Nepalese refugee camp to a west Texan housing project. Other times I walked alongside friends who were changing jobs, careers, or degrees.

Once I stumbled on this theme of walking alongside people, or of *journeying* with others, I saw it everywhere. Life began to make sense. I realized that teaching, whether in Spanish middle schools or in refugee resettlement agencies, is about hospitality and journeying with students for a semester, a year, or a season. I realized that meeting people who were facing eviction and working with them to make phone calls, collect checks from charities, and negotiate with landlords is really just about meeting people where they are and walking with them through a difficult season—even though, in that job, I usually saw those people for only one afternoon. Writing and editing projects allowed me to journey alongside people I did not even know.

I realized that being open to see and meet people and to walk with them for a while is a gift I am able to give in a unique way. This is the theme of my life. This is the way God knit my life together. All the days of my life, even the ones that didn't seem to fit, were woven together with these threads before my first breath. This is my calling.

Other people have other themes. My husband's theme and calling is *equipping others*. He is fabulous at breaking down complex ideas and explaining them in fresh and accessible ways. The fact that his theme, his calling, is equipping means that the period of time he spent before and during seminary working with teens and young adults at a frozen yogurt shop wasn't wasted time. He was living out his calling even then as he taught them—both how to properly clean out the yogurt machines for the fifth time and how to more fully embrace being an adult in this world.

His theme of equipping also plays out in his love of preaching, even if he doesn't do it often. My husband's theme of equipping is why he mentors teens in our church's youth ministry. His theme is the reason you can find him meeting with various people throughout the week to explain the best way to structure a sermon or the best way to parallel park. His theme of equipping is why eventually he would like to get a PhD and teach formal theological education.

His theme flows out of him. He equips no matter his surrounding. It's his calling.

Themes help us make sense of our lives' big picture and bring in the outliers. When I think about my life in terms of theme, everything fits. Even the jobs I have done that weren't overtly spiritual enough to be considered "ministry" still fit with my theme. I didn't have the tools to explain how those jobs fit my calling at the time, but I knew I was living into my calling. Looking back, my theme makes sense of those times.

There were other times when I worked jobs that didn't seem to fit into the trajectory of my long-term ministry goals. I felt like I was good at those jobs and had something to offer. I longed to feel validated in those positions, but I didn't have the model or the language to integrate my experiences into the larger picture of my calling. But now I do.

Understanding my calling as a theme has also helped me to move forward and make decisions. I'm chronically bad at making decisions. I have always struggled with predicting which college, major, city, or job will be the best fit for me. I used to worry about taking jobs or engaging opportunities that might send me down a ministry path that was not my own.

Now I have a filter for these opportunities. In addition to looking for arrows, I ask myself whether the opportunity fits my theme. Could

I journey with other people in that situation? No? Then I pass. But if I can journey with people in those situations, I give the opportunities a second thought. This model of understanding my calling allows me to engage in ministry opportunities that I might not have previously realized were a part of my calling.

After my AmeriCorps service year in Denver ended, I was looking for a job in all kinds of social services agencies. I looked at work in churches and with nonprofits. In the end, I was offered a position as an office manager for a start-up business. Initially, the job didn't interest me. I can't be the only one who is plagued by questions like *Did I go to seminary so that I could be an office manager?* Those are the kinds of ugly blisters that pop up when I am not operating under a model of calling that fits and gives me the freedom to be myself.

I started evaluating that opportunity in terms of my theme. Would I be journeying with people? Surprisingly, when I asked that question, I realized that my answer was yes. I was invited to be part of a company, a start-up, founded by two people who were formally in youth ministry. They were trying to use a business to support themselves and also to bring change to the world—primarily by facilitating outdoor adventure retreats but also by donating to and partnering with a group of nonprofits.

I realized that my random assortment of gifts and areas of expertise would allow me to walk alongside these people as they frantically worked on the details necessary to get a start-up company off the ground. I wrote press releases, I prayed in staff meetings, and I sent packing lists to fathers and daughters. I walked businessmen through our online forms, and I met with our nonprofit partners. When my boss got frazzled, I showed up with Reese's peanut butter cups.

In the end, I spent nine months working in that office, doing a variety of jobs in exchange for tiny paychecks. Eventually I no longer felt comfortable in my role and decided to move on. The job didn't end well. The experience was difficult, but I still think it was part of my calling. Previously, I might have walked away and said that it was wasted time or that I probably should have been doing ministry instead. Armed with the knowledge that my calling, my *theme*, is journeying with others, however, I realize that the difficult journey we walked together was ministry. It was hard. But it was a part of my calling.

I enjoy talking to people about what their own themes might be. I like looking for patterns, and I know that this is part of the reason themes appeal to me so much. I love to ask people what makes their heart soar and what hard work they will dig into because it's worth it to them. I hate to hear people talk about how they swam against the current of their callings, but I think that hearing about what doesn't work—the ways of living that damage our sense of self and sense of purpose in God's kingdom—is also a way to understand what we *are* called to do.

Themes are varied, just like the people called to them. A friend of mine has not given a formal name to her theme, but I think it is encouragement. She encourages women—women who are struggling to find jobs, women who are growing children inside of them, women in formal ministry positions, and women in the pews. She mails handwritten cards and sends care packages that arrive on the worst of days. She networks and writes and speaks and preaches, but her core intent and purpose is to encourage others. She brings people together so that they can encourage each other. She teaches her students and encourages them along the way. She spots hidden talents and desires in people and pulls those gifts to the surface. She is the reason my story is a book.

Theme also helps us talk about calling in a way that encompasses our entire lives. What is so hard for me to internalize, especially when I feel weak or invalidated, is that *calling* is not synonymous with *career*. Our calling does not equal our job. Our job does not equal our calling. The idea that our calling is not the same as our job is fairly easy to grasp mentally, but it is harder to internalize. We have spent so many decades talking about calling in terms of careers—a calling to be a missionary, a preacher, an elementary school teacher—that it is hard for many of us to unseat this model. Unfortunately, the marriage of calling and career can lead to damage and disappointment.

In our current economic situation in which jobs are hard to come by, and full-time or salaried ministry jobs are even more rare, how do we speak about calling to the crowds of newly graduated college or seminary students who struggle to find meaningful employment? Have they misheard their calling if they can't find a paid job in a pulpit? What do we say to the minister whose church members feel like they have no other recourse but to cut staff positions? Is this just the loss of a job, or is it also the loss of a calling?

There's a difficulty, too, in uniting *calling* and *career* in family life. If a parent decides to leave the workforce to care for a newborn child or an aging parent, is she still able to live out her calling? If we were to look at a church member who is caring for an aging parent more than forty hours a week, would we tell him that his work is not true ministry? I don't think we would. I think we know that caring for others—the young, the aging, the mentally ill, the sick, or the differently abled—is a true act of ministry. We live out our calling most fully when we are serving these people who are often on the margins of society.

We take at least one day a year to praise moms and dads and their hard work of parenting. Yet I know many full-time moms who feel like they have had to abandon their calling in order to do this work. They love being moms and the extra and important time they spend with their kids, but how do they reconcile their calling when they don't have careers?

Thinking about ministry and calling as career is full of pitfalls. I know these pitfalls well. I have felt relieved when I have had a "ministry" job to share when people ask me what I do. I also know the somewhat inexplicable urge I have felt to contextualize the work I have done outside the church. When I worked as an office manager, I felt the need to tell people that I was gaining business experience working with a start-up so that one day I could minister by doing economic development in a less developed country.

Why do I feel the need to make these kinds of explanations?

The uncomfortable truth is that I have so internalized career and calling as a pair that I struggle for validation in my calling when I work in a less-than-ideal job situation. Ironically, I have had "ministry" jobs that allowed me much less space to flourish in my calling than when I taught high school students English verb tenses. At the time

I couldn't see that I could be living into my calling right in the middle of a secular job.

Another problem with viewing calling as career is that we don't stay in our careers forever. At the downtown church where I worked in Denver, most of my volunteers were in their sixties or seventies, with some even well into their eighties. Many of them had been in social work or held staff positions at churches. As they transitioned into retirement, they grappled with where and how their callings still applied. As such a vast portion of our population begins to enter retirement, how will we help them continue to live into their callings? We can't do that by tying calling to a job.

Our callings last our whole lives. Our callings are bigger than our jobs. Our callings are bigger than our unemployment, and they are bigger than our underemployment. Our callings seep like tea into the water of our whole lives. They flavor everything.

Thinking about calling as career is like wearing wet, constricting boots. Even if that model feels like it fits us for now, it may not in five or ten or fifteen years. While thinking of our calling as a job might seem like it's working for us, we should know that it's not working for some of our colleagues and peers. It's not working for people in areas of the country and world who find their occupational options limited. And, if the model of seeing a calling as a career seems to make us feel good about our selves and our callings, we might need to take a hard look at where we are searching for and receiving validation.

I think we can do better than thinking of calling as a job. I find it hard to break from that model, but I know that when I do, I appreciate that my calling can be expressed my entire life, in all areas of my life. I can see coffee dates with friends not as wasting time or even as mere leisure, but as an important way for me to journey with others. Being present with others is a gift I am uniquely able to offer. Not only is it important for me to do these things; it would impoverish others and myself not to share it.

With an understanding of my calling as a theme that weaves through all aspects of my life, I also don't have to worry about the worthy jobs and important tasks that don't fit inside my theme. I used to struggle with all the things I *could do*. How do I decide what I should do when there are so many options and so many worthy causes?

Understanding my calling as a theme that runs throughout my life, unique to me and my experiences, frees me from the guilt of everything I *could* do. My ability with math and science at a young age might have meant that I could have made it through medical school, but it would not have been a good fit for my personality or good stewardship of the way God has made me. We need surgeons in this world, but we also need people with the calling God has given me—a calling that sometimes means sitting and listening to stories of the young, old, or drunk.

Understanding my theme helps me say no to good things that are outside of my gifting. It helps me to find satisfaction and purpose in work that might seem unimportant to others.

Finally, understanding my calling as a theme, and separating it from a calling to one specific career, means that I can embrace a new western world that seems to be moving away from a culture in which lifelong careers exist. I remember the first time I heard someone quote a statistic that said most in my generation would not have lifelong careers. Instead, they would have four to five different jobs across their working lifetimes. At least career-wise, I think author Barbara Kingsolver is right when she says, "Everyone of us is called upon, probably many times, to start a new life."[1] Understanding our calling as a lifelong theme, maybe to be practiced in a number of different careers, better prepares us to make the required starts, stops, and transitions.

In the end, God made us, and God called us. Embracing a model of calling that values our whole lives and our whole beings celebrates that. We are able to pry off the old models that aren't prepared to handle our entire journey and continue to walk onward, even through the rain.

As I walked through the stormy meseta, and as I have continued to follow the winding path of my calling, I have had lots of time to think about the models we have been using to talk about calling. I have learned about pain and rain, about boots and blisters. I have learned to question assumptions about the way things are "supposed to be." Most of all, I have learned to give myself the freedom to choose a different way—a way that fits.

Note

1. *High Tide in Tucson: Essays from Now or Never* (New York: Harper Perennial, 1996) 15.

Chapter 8

León–Remembering Why We Are Doing This

I was putting in long days to get to León. It was the next major city along the pilgrimage, marking the end of the meseta and the beginning of the last third of my journey to Santiago. I hiked a little extra each day, trying to make up a couple days' worth of hiking to get to León by Sunday.

Normally, a day or two would not make a difference in my timeline. I had gotten into the habit of walking until I was tired and stopping for the day, with a few exceptions. León was an exception. I wanted to get there by Sunday because Sunday was Easter, and Easter in Spain is something to behold.

Spaniards have a long and complicated history with the church. After almost forty years of the last century under a dictator who used Spain's Catholic Church to manipulate and extend even more control over the population, the religious atmosphere in Spain is different from what it was for centuries before. Spain was once one of the most Catholic countries in the world, but modern Spain has moved towards secularism and away from the church that shaped its history.

Throughout most of my previous time in Spain, my experience with Spain's churches—from the magnificent Spanish cathedrals to the small Romanesque churches—was more akin to visiting fascinating museums than attending church. The buildings were beautiful but largely empty. The spaces felt sacred but forgotten.

At that point, I had attended pilgrim Masses at just about any church that offered them along my walk. There was a beautiful Mass in Estella with a young priest who called all pilgrims to the front of the church before the Eucharist. He surveyed the native countries and languages of the half dozen of us who gathered. He blessed us in Spanish, in English, and in Portuguese and gave us prayer cards to take along with us.

The pilgrims' Mass in Estella left a surprising mark on me. I felt supported and understood in a journey that few people understand—even the people who loved me and wanted to support me. Still, when our multinational group of pilgrims returned to our pews, we were in the company of only a handful of elderly Spanish women. The Masses in all the Spanish cathedrals and churches along the way had seemed to attract pilgrims, but not many other people.

During my walk through the meseta, my interactions with Spanish churches changed. Walking through the meseta was different, not just because of the flatness or the rain. It was different because I hiked through that region during holy week.

Modern-day Spain may not be very religious on an everyday basis, but on a deep national level, Spain shows up for Easter and the holy week that leads up to it like no one else. I had heard and read about the way Spain celebrated Easter, but I had yet to experience it in person.

Having the opportunity to make a pilgrimage that included such a sacred time in the church's calendar helped me make the decision to do the Camino when I did. I wanted to see Spain's elaborate street parades and processions. I wanted to see the altar pieces turned into parade floats that groups of people would carry on their backs, their steps synchronized to the beating of a drum. I wanted to see the processions of men dressed in robes and streams of women dressed as mourners in black. I wanted to hear the trumpets wail through the streets and feel the crowds of people huddle around me.

I wanted to experience Easter in Spain, and I wanted to do it in León. Founded during Roman times, León is the largest city of the region. It would be my first city since leaving Burgos. León also has one of Spain's most beautiful cathedrals. I wanted to be there on Easter morning with the other people of the area, all of us celebrating together.

Arriving in León by Easter was getting harder by the day. The long hikes were wearing on me. My right ankle was swelling more and more. Still, I put my head down and walked, especially since I was largely walking my way through the meseta alone. I was making progress, but León was still in the distance.

The Saturday before Easter, I had to make a decision. I limped my way into Mansilla, the town just before León on the Camino, by late afternoon. As stubborn as I am, I was willing to concede that my swollen ankle was not looking good. I knew I couldn't walk any further that afternoon. Easter was the next day, and I hadn't made it to León.

I debated taking a taxi from Mansilla into León that evening or the next morning. I wanted to be there in time to see the processions that began at dawn. And, with my stubbornness kicking in, I considered just sucking it up and hiking the brief stretch into the city on foot that evening. Still unsure of what to do, I walked to Mansilla's pilgrim hostel.

Decision-making is not my strength when I am at my best, but at the end of the long day, I couldn't make up my mind. I polled the people I knew in the hostel and decided to ask the volunteer running the hostel what she thought. By that point, I was leaning towards staying for the night but unsure whether to walk or take a taxi the next day.

As I went to the reception area, the door of the hostel opened and almost hit me. I couldn't believe who came in! It was my retired Sevillian friend, Juanma. I hadn't seen him or his wife Maica since Burgos, when I left for my weekend trip to the north. I thought they would be days ahead of me, but I had caught up to them. Right after that, I saw my friend Sylvia from Germany, whom I also hadn't seen for days. Seeing these friends solved my dilemma. I would stay the night. On top of that, Sylvia offered me a place in a taxi she was sharing with a couple of other pilgrims into León the next morning. She said we could split the cost and be there in time to see the Easter morning activities. I still felt unsure about taking a taxi into León, feeling that maybe I should walk, when Maica reminded me that we need Sabbath even on pilgrimages. I was sold!

Early the next morning, I gathered with Sylvia and her friends and piled into a taxi headed for León. Once we got into town, we followed the sound of drums and the people dressed in traditional costumes to find the beginning of the Easter processions. We got to watch the start of the parade with hardly anyone around.

I felt a bit guilty taking a taxi into town, even though it wasn't too far. However, I knew it was the best choice for my ankle and also the only way I would get to see the processions, which were a highlight of the entire Camino for me. The long days and the pain and swelling in my right ankle were worth it to spend Easter in León.

People marched through the city in elaborate robes and hoods, carrying heavy sculptures of Easter scenes. Two separate processions met in front of the impressive gothic cathedral to culminate the celebration—the sculptures of Jesus and the empty tomb met the procession of Mary and the grieving women. The people carrying the sculptures, which were essentially altarpieces, made them "dance" by causing the scenes to sway back and forth as they carried them on their backs.

All the people of the city started clapping. A small sermon and prayer were broadcast from the cathedral into the plaza where we all stood shoulder to shoulder. The sermon was in Spanish, and I don't remember and didn't understand every word. What I do remember was the priest speaking through the loud speakers of the cathedral, reminding us again and again: The night is over. Death is over. Peace and love have won.

Peace and love have won. At that moment, they released hundreds of doves from the towers of the cathedral. All of us in the crowd began to clap as our hearts swelled together.

Love has won. All the pain and long days were worth it. It was worth it to experience Easter in León. It was worth it to be part of the swell of emotion that comes with celebrating the sacred in a crowd of strangers fused together for a moment in time. It was also worth it to make it to León, in all the wetness and pain it took to get there, to be reminded of why I decided to take this long, hard walk in the first place.

I needed to remember the nature of the journey I was on. I needed to remember why I was on a pilgrimage. I needed to remember how my story was going to end—that it would end with love and peace winning.

I easily become forgetful when days get long. I am ashamed to admit that I can get lost in the grind and not remember the *why* of much of anything I do. Busy lives do that to us. Sometimes I can only check off the long list of tasks in front of me if I allow myself to transition into what I call "machine mode." But becoming a machine is no way to live.

Machine mode is something I have seen happen again and again, not just in individuals but also in organizations and ministries. When there is a big job to do, no one is immune from losing sight of the vision behind what they are doing.

One of the nonprofits I worked with serves homeless people in downtown Denver. Our participants also struggled with other obstacles—mental illnesses, addictions, unregulated medical issues such as diabetes, lack of high school diplomas, illiteracy, and so on. Our organization's goal was to provide some meaningful work and community for these individuals while paying them a stipend for their work to help offset some of their expenses. We had anywhere from forty-five to fifty-five individuals in the program at any given time.

Like every other aid organization in our city, we were overwhelmed. We did not have enough staff, enough funding, or enough space—we actually had a storage space that was affectionately and officially called the "scary closet." We rounded up all interns and volunteers we could find, but we didn't have the time or staff to do anything but basic training with them. We scrambled to enroll new clients and offer new, more comprehensive services all while struggling to provide our core services well.

We couldn't take a breath and look up. There was so much to do. It was hard to focus on our vision statement when we also needed to find someone to disinfect the bathroom and someone else to give a participant a ride to pick up his medication before the pharmacy closed for the weekend. We scrambled to open our doors to the larger community as well but didn't realize how thin we had already spread ourselves.

Our problem wasn't just that we were spread thin. Our larger problem was that we did not remember who we were as an organization or what we were created to do. We were too busy getting good things—necessary things!—done to remember who we were. We had forgotten where we had come from and didn't know where we were headed. We just knew we needed more donations to buy a new property, more volunteers to work craft fairs the next weekend, and someone to tend to the smoking stove in the workshop.

What we needed was time to focus. We needed to create time and space for ourselves, not just to catch up on paperwork but also to remember the community we were serving. We needed time to deepen our vision as an organization and re-center the work we were doing more concretely around that vision. We were doing work that was outside our area of expertise or beyond our capacity. We needed to delegate some of the work to other groups and organizations in the city.

We needed space to cast a vision for the future and think about how to get there. As an organization, we needed to look up, we needed to look back, and we needed to look forward.

The problem of looking up is not limited to organizations. I can spot organizations that are blind to their original and greater purpose so much more clearly than I can diagnose the same problem within my own life and attitudes. But these habits often find their way into my life. I find it hard to stop. I find it hard to look up.

Many people who work in ministry and social services get burned out. Sometimes the burnout is a low flame that, over time, finally leaves us charred and surprised. Other times the burnout comes on quickly and either numbs us or sends us packing to a different profession. Whichever way burnout approaches me, I have trouble squelching the flame. I have trouble seeing it coming.

Part of my problem is that I want to be present to each individual in front of me. I want to help everyone! I want to be able to counsel friends *and* make call after call until I find an organization that will offer rental assistance to the person who showed up at my office after we ran out of funds. I want to cook dinner each night *and* make quarterly statistics reports complete with graphs. I want to be able to solve homelessness *and* poverty *and* human trafficking *and* unhappiness.

When I look up, I know that I am crazy. There is no doubting it. There is no possible way to do all of those things (or even *any* of those things some days). I can see that when I look up and remember why I am pursuing my calling. My problem is that I don't remember to look up. Sometimes I don't even remember *how* to look up!

It's like finding myself with a stretch of thirty-kilometer days ahead of me, walking with busted ankles, swollen feet, and blistered toes. I keep trudging ahead because momentum and duty carry me forward. I am lost in the details but marching onward, with my head down and my nose to the grindstone.

Machine mode. It leaves us all busted, bruised, and burned out. I've had to learn the hard way that we are not machines. We are bodies and spirits and image bearers of God. We are members of a larger collection of bodies and spirits and images that become a community, a church, a body. We are made to be part of a body, not to be machines—even if we are machines in the service of a worthy cause.

Staying out of the trap of productivity, especially in Western cultures, is difficult. How do we do it? I'm not sure, but I think it has something to do with that cathedral in León, those processions through the street, and the doves released with the announcement that *peace and love have won.* I don't think this is a trap we dig ourselves out of. I think it is a release we have to keep accepting again and again. Looking up and finding grace is the way out of our predicament.

As I walked, especially over the vacant paths through the vast meseta toward León, I thought about the pilgrims who had walked the same ground over the past thousand years. I wondered why they walked. I wondered if they walked for forgiveness. I wondered if they put one foot in front of the other, blister after blister, in order to receive grace—for themselves or for others.

I admire the faith of these pilgrims, but it also breaks my heart. The opening lines of Mary Oliver's poem, *Wild Geese,* echoed through my ears as I walked.

You do not have to be good.
You do not have to walk on your knees
for a hundred miles through the desert, repenting.

The gospel story agrees. God's grace and Jesus' work are complete without my dusty steps in the desert. God's work in conquering our mistakes and limitations, in our past and our future, is complete. God's work is finished. I don't need to accrue any new blisters or serve ten more people a nutritious breakfast to earn that grace. My life has meaning and redemption through the life and death and life again of Jesus the Messiah—not through Jesus the Messiah *and* my well-prepared Sunday school lesson. Not through my Jesus *and* my spreadsheet complete with graphs. Not through Jesus *and* my tidy kitchen, my smooth-running nonprofit, my moving sermon, or the miles I have walked.

Jesus is enough.

Thank God.

Living into the reality of grace is not easy, though. The clacking of my walking stick compels me like a metronome to keep moving, to keep going, to keep doing, and to keep searching. How do we stop and look up? How do we remember why we are on a pilgrimage?

One way I have learned to stop and look up is through engaging spiritual disciplines. These help me to remember who I am, where I am headed on my journey into my calling, and why I am traveling. If we get too busy doing work, even good work, we will forget why we are pursuing our calling. Spiritual disciplines can help us remember and help us keep looking up.

I have found several disciplines, from inside and from outside my faith tradition, to be helpful in different seasons and stages of my life. Much like taking a five-hundred-mile hike, developing a spiritual practice requires putting one foot in front of the other. We start small, and we keep doing it.

Spiritual disciplines can be anything from reading the Bible or other spiritual books to feeding the poor, fasting, or keeping prayer beads in a pocket. Spiritual disciplines are anything that we actively engage in that gives us space to see God at work around us. Spiritual disciplines can be formal, creative, traditional, or modern.

Different spiritual disciplines attract different people. Sometimes certain disciplines are useful in different periods of our lives. A variety of spiritual disciplines can help us look up and keep our focus and perspective.

One of the most helpful disciplines I have encountered is that of gratitude. The spiritual practice of gratitude has time and again pulled my head up from the ground, from my productive impulse, and allowed me to feel afresh the grace that sustains me on the journey of my calling.

I actually came across the idea of thinking of gratitude as a spiritual discipline the year I lived and worked in downtown Denver. That year of service, and all it entailed, was the most emotionally draining season of my life so far. I was grappling, with limited tools, with how to survive that season without resorting to my old enemy named burnout. I knew that my calling had brought me to those positions, but I could feel myself sliding into my old pattern. I could feel machine mode take over some days.

My days were so full and my energy stores so low that I felt machine mode might be my only option. I wanted to be emotionally present to all the people I saw at work who were in various stages of crisis and isolation. I wanted to be a stable and welcoming space to my housemates at the time, who were all struggling with processing their service assignments along with walking through times of transition and self-discovery in their personal journeys.

I wanted to journey with people. I wanted to lean into my calling and walk beside them. But I also didn't want to work so hard that I lost focus of who I was and why I was walking that hard road to begin with. I needed more tools.

In one of our daily reflection times at my morning job, we watched a brief video that another staff member had chosen. Each week we picked some kind of inspirational or educational material to read or watch with all the participants. The idea was that our participants, all of whom had experienced or were currently enduring homelessness, would have space to express their thoughts and feelings while building community.

Over all, our reflection times included bright moments of insight. Participants generally liked having a moment to sit and listen. Others enjoyed being listened to. By this point in the year, though, reflection time had become just another obstacle to get through.

The video that day was a two and a half minute portion of an interview with professor and researcher Brené Brown. She was talking about how gratitude is a practice that can change our lives.

We have all heard about gratitude. We know we are supposed to be thankful, and we know that we should be thankful in months other than November. I was generally a thankful person. When I sat down to think about it, I knew that I had heaps of things to be grateful for. What I didn't know was that gratitude isn't just a realization I should come to every now and then. Instead, gratitude is best practiced as a discipline. In fact, I came to realize that gratitude is a *spiritual* discipline.

On my first viewing of this clip, I was intrigued by Brown's spin on gratitude. I liked the idea of practicing it regularly, and she noted that the people her research showed to be the most grateful were not the people with the easiest lives. The people who were the most grateful were the ones who actively chose to be grateful. Being content doesn't make us grateful. Being grateful makes us content.

I watched Brown's video three times that week, each with a different set of participants. Her ideas slowly started growing roots, and by the third day's viewing, I was officially thinking about how I could practice gratitude as a discipline in my life. She had mentioned that some of the people she interviewed made a habit of saying aloud something they were grateful for each evening, or wrote down things they were thankful for in a journal. One thing that struck me was that some of her research participants made it a goal to be thankful at specific times throughout the day.

I was interested. The fact that the season of Lent, the time in the church calendar during which spiritual disciplines are most embraced and encouraged, was just around the corner probably spurred me on. I decided to put my smart phone, almost always tucked into my back pocket, to use for something other than texting and Google maps. I picked three times—one in the morning, one during lunch, and one in the early evening—when I would not typically be at my desk or in a meeting, and I set alarms. I named the alarms "Gratitude."

Three times a day, my phone buzzed in my pocket or purse and reminded me to be grateful. It was a simple discipline that changed my life in profound ways.

In the beginning, I was grateful for the things that come to mind first for most people. I was thankful for my family. I was thankful for my friends. I was thankful for my health and for waking up that morning.

The people I was around also shaped my gratitude. Spending my days with people who were struggling through homelessness or in need of emergency financial assistance, I was thankful to have housing. I was thankful, especially in the evenings, to have a roof over my head and a warm meal on the table. I was thankful to have money to pay my rent, and I was thankful that if I needed three dollars to pay a prescription copay, I could easily scrounge it up.

By setting alarms, gratitude also broke into my day. My phone would begin to buzz and chime in my pocket, and I would look up at the friend in front of me. I gave voice to my gratitude for that person. The practice started to change the way I viewed my relationship with him or her. Frequently I found myself with expanding gratefulness for my housemates and for David, who is now my husband.

I'll admit that at other times I struggled. I didn't always want to be grateful. Some days, thick into a season in which I felt physically sick almost constantly, in which I was emotionally weighed down by the trauma of others around me, and was more often than not covered in a layer food scraps from the soup kitchen, I resented the expectation that I was supposed to be grateful. On some of those days, the alarm would sound as I shuffled home, with barely enough energy to pick my feet up one after the other, and I would be thankful that the day was over. That's all I had in me.

Still, the habit began to take root. I knew the alarms were coming, so I made note of my surroundings as the mornings and afternoons came to a close. I began to notice the lavender growing on the side of the road. I noted that I had an especially cheerful bus driver. I realized that the socks I wore were doing an exceptional job at keeping my feet warm. I began to stockpile gratitude.

In the midst of the thankfulness that started to build up inside me, I began to let things go—and I was grateful for that. I began to see God in the hard days, and I was able to say, "I'm thankful that you are in charge of that problem." "I'm thankful that you love that person more than I ever could." "I'm grateful that, in the midst of craziness and trauma, I have love and grace in my life."

I also began to let go some of the things I couldn't change. It's harder to be mad about the little negative parts of life—like the unshoveled snow on the sidewalks, the housemates who left out dishes *again*, the fact that I needed to fill my car with gas when I was already running late—when I am forcing myself to thank God for the little positive parts of life, like the fact that no one saw me wipe out spectacularly while walking on the unshoveled sidewalk, or the one housemate who reliably starts the dishwasher *and* manages to smile in the mornings.

I've found God in the big and little blessings in my life, just the same as I have found God in the big and little traumas of this world. God is there just the same. Gratefulness was my pathway to that truth and to joy. There's joy in knowing we aren't in control and that someone greater than us is. There's joy in knowing the Creator delights in me and, like me, also delights in little purple crocus flowers at the first sign of spring.

The spiritual discipline of gratitude was my pathway to prayer. It was a gateway to recognizing my place in the world, and it was a joyful reminder of why I was doing all that I did. At my darkest moments, gratitude also helped me remember that despite what my surroundings looked like, in some mysterious way, peace and love have already won.

Spiritual disciplines can do that. They can bring our purpose and our circumstances into the gracious light of God's larger plan. We can re-recognize why we are enduring the struggle. We can even stop for a few moments during the struggle and look up to search for the

Divine. Spiritual disciplines remind us how our callings, our daily tasks, and God's plan for the world all work together.

Following our callings will no doubt take us down some busy, painful roads. Finding ourselves tired and slipping towards burnout is easy to do, even when we are following our callings. Sometimes we are called right into the middle of the world's messes. Other times, our callings collide with other people's paths of destruction. How do we survive? How do we look up?

Spiritual disciplines help us remember why we are pursuing our calling. They help us avoid burnout. For me, the practice of gratitude, even going to the extreme of setting alarms, restored my joy and reminded me that God is in charge. It reminded me that I walked the journey I was on, and that I journeyed with others, because of gratefulness for forgiveness, love, and the Easter story. I needed that reminder. In fact, I needed that reminder at seven, noon, and five.

We are all instructed to give thanks and be joyful, but there are other practices that give us space to see God and remember our place in God's story. I know people who pray the hours along with monks the world over, and I know people who recalibrate their lives using a daily examen from the Ignatian tradition. These practices have helped Christians connect with the Creator for centuries.

Other people I know take more creative approaches. I know people who pray and center themselves by coloring mandelas. I know people who paint elaborate canvases and people who doodle their prayers in journals. Others walk labyrinths or even just trace images of labyrinths with their fingers.

We can reach outside of our traditions, too. A conservative evangelical pastor I know loves to pray with Catholic prayer beads in his pocket. I know Catholics who like to meditate on God's grace by singing black spirituals. Colleagues of mine take quarterly days of silence and solitude. Others use practices ranging from yoga to good old-fashioned quiet times. Spiritual disciplines help to pull us out of our own muck, out of the wet or dusty paths right in front of us. They help us remember why we walk the paths of our callings.

Our daily paths may be full of consuming tasks and long days, but spiritual disciplines point us to something bigger. Like taking a taxi into León to see parades of the faithful marching toward the cathedral, carrying hundred-pound statues on their shared backs, they remind us of what the larger path we are walking on is about. The larger path is about grace and forgiveness. The larger path reminds us that peace has won. The larger path repeats that, no matter how much we get done, love has finished the job.

Chapter 9

Galicia—The Mountains Get Bigger and So Do Our Muscles

About a week after León, I began my pilgrimage through Galicia, the westernmost region of Spain. Galicia, which makes up a part of Spain that is known as Celtic Spain, is the extreme opposite of the austere and expansive meseta. It is mountainous and green, mystical and lush.

After resting for two full days in León—the first day to celebrate Easter and the next to take in León's beautiful monasteries, architecture, and pharmacies—I felt refreshed. My ankle looked better, and the swelling had gone down considerably. My spirit was revived by the Easter celebrations.

Feeling rested, I was off again. I was more or less two-thirds of the way to Santiago. By that time, I felt as if I had been walking and making that journey for my entire life. It seemed unbelievable that I had a third of the pilgrimage left. This was unbelievable both because it seemed impossible that I *still* had so many miles left to walk after such an extended journey and because all of a sudden my arrival in Santiago felt imminent.

It also seemed unbelievable because I had planned to have myself sorted out by the time I got to Santiago. I was decidedly not yet sorted. So I packed up my backpack in León, and I hit the trail yet again.

Walking through Galicia put an extra pep in my step. I was excited to pass through the final region of the Camino. The landscape is undeniably beautiful. In spring, the trees along the path formed green tunnels, and the hillsides were covered in purple and yellow wildflowers. The fog shaded the surrounding mountains, coloring everything in the distance in different shades of slate blue.

Making a pilgrimage through Galicia put to test all the pilgrim lessons I had learned so far. Green mountain landscapes are beautiful to look at, but they require two things to make them so lovely: rain and inclines. My time in Galicia was filled with both of those.

Some inclines and mountains were larger than others, some were steeper, and some were more beautiful, but my days of walking on flat surfaces were over. I had to reach back into my repertoire and remember how I got myself up Alto de Perdón and all the other mountains I had climbed before reaching the meseta. The mountains of Galicia provided a constant up, down, and up again. They were ubiquitous, but one particular mountain, Alto do Poio, made me nervous.

The day I climbed Alto do Poio, I had been walking with my Sevillian friends again. They left earlier than I did that morning, but I caught up with them before lunch. The path we walked took us higher and higher with each bend. Soon we were walking through the clouds. We moved in single file, with Juanma up ahead of us and barely visible in the fog. The thick air on my skin, the excitement of making it to our final region, and the mysterious spirit of Galicia gave the view a fairytale-like tint.

The path finally leveled out into the stone-covered town of O Cebreiro. Our first stop was the town's almost thousand-year-old Romanesque church in the square. The church was built on the foundations of an earlier church that dated to centuries before that. My friends and I leaned our walking sticks on the wall outside the church and made a circuit inside the small, dark building.

At the back of the church, we got stamps for our Camino passports, and I picked up a second passport. My original pilgrim passport was almost out of space. All those steps, all those nights in pilgrim hostels, all those long days in the sun were adding up. I was getting somewhere.

We rejoined our hiking sticks and followed the yellow arrows through town, making it up the hill just outside O Cebreiro as the clouds started to break. We stopped and rested on the base of a pilgrim statue. I passed around a bag of dried apricots, and we all ate handfuls. We'd need all the energy we could get for the tough climb ahead of us.

Alto do Poio had weighed on our minds for a few days. Many pilgrims carry pieces of paper that show elevation changes for each day or stage on the Camino. The up and down that happened between O Cebreiro and Alto do Poio made us nervous. The climb up Alto do Poio was the steepest of the entire pilgrimage. Sometimes referred to as the "roof of the Camino," this mountain is the highest point of the entire pilgrimage. We had heard of a lady who was determined to make it up Alto do Poio and resorted to climbing up on all fours. Once we saw the mountain for ourselves, her idea didn't seem so outrageous.

The whole climb was difficult, but the last part was almost vertical. I had picked up an extra walking stick the day before to help propel me upward. I practically pulled myself up that mountain. Maica and I went slowly and cheered ourselves onward by remembering all the other mountains we had climbed and all the other feats we had accomplished thus far.

Juanma was waiting and cheering for us from the café on top of the mountain. When we made it, Maica bought us all a celebratory round of juice, and Juanma signed us into the café's guestbook to document the fact that, yes, we conquered Alto do Poio! From then on, Alto do Poio became our rallying cry. If we could make it up Alto do Poio, we could do anything!

Galicia gave us lots of opportunities to test ourselves. We went up hills, we went down mountains, and we climbed inclines like Alto do Poio. The final section of our pilgrimage was so different from the initial climb I had made up Alto de Perdón in the first days outside Pamplona. At this latter point of the journey, my climbing was no longer powered by adrenaline and excitement as it was in the beginning. After weeks of paring down the items I carried, the pack on my back was precisely no lighter and no heavier than necessary—and I was used to carrying it. I walked with aches, but I was accustomed to enduring the pain and walking through it. I had also learned to recognize when the pain was a signal that I needed a break.

By the time I got to Galicia, the inclines were bigger, but so were my muscles. I had developed what I lovingly referred to as my mountain goat muscles. I would come around the bend of a path, see a hill in front of me, and switch gears—taking bigger steps, widening my stance a bit, and letting my muscles do the work. I actually began to enjoy climbing the mountains. I was fascinated and proud of the muscles that could easily pull me up a mountain with all my belongings on my back.

I believe that as we journey into our calling, we experience something similar to trekking through Galicia. I don't think it is helpful to say or hear that things will get easier as you go. Sometimes, most times even, as we journey into our callings, things do not get easier. What happens is that we get stronger. We get braver. We get more resilient. And we don't get to any of those points by taking the bus from city to city; we get to them by climbing the mountains and overcoming obstacles again and again.

For me, one of the bigger mountains in life has been conflict. I thought that if I were following the correct path of my calling, I would experience little conflict. I do not like conflict. I never have. I grew up in a very loving environment, and I never learned how to deal with, let alone engage in, conflict. Avoiding conflict served me well for a while. I was thankful to be in jobs and relationships for years that were relatively free of conflict. It seemed that many people had soaked up the same lessons on conflict that I had: avoid it.

Eventually, conflict arose. Without tools to deal with it, the people around me and I resorted to avoidance, blame, guilt, and all the other unhealthy tools we reach for in fear and discomfort. Those reactions are never productive.

In the years since, I have read books on leadership and conflict, and I even took a conflict management class in seminary. While helpful, they still did not make conflict easier to handle. What made conflict easier to handle, even engage in, was walking through it. Again and again.

Within the last year, I had to leave a job. I had never quit a job before. I had left when it was time for me to move to new cities or continents, but never because I didn't feel like I could work there anymore. I felt like my calling had led me to this particular job, but I eventually became aware that my position no longer gave me room to live out of my calling.

Leaving was particularly complicated because my husband and I knew my boss before I accepted the position. We had lots of friends in common. While the job had not been ideal for me, I felt that I was able to use my random assortment of skills to journey with my boss in a new start-up company. I had wanted to learn more about business, especially the ways to combine business and ministry, and this opening seemed like the right opportunity at the time. I would be able journey with others and also learn new skills that I might be able to use as the trajectory of my calling continued to evolve.

In the end, the job was fine. It paid the bills, though without much left over. It gave me the emotional space to recover from an intense year of serving alongside Denver's working poor and living in community with other aid workers. I liked that I could set boundaries and not take my work home with me. I liked that I was able to bridge gaps and walk alongside others in the company, even when it meant doing tedious tasks.

Eventually, though, what started out as a somewhat complex relationship with my boss turned toxic for me. The way he interacted with others and with me didn't line up with the values he had set up for himself or with my values. I started to worry that the whole experience was a mistake. I found myself thinking that I should have never taken the job in the first place.

What I had to remember was that following my calling did not mean my life would be easy or get easier. Following the arrows of my calling did not mean I wouldn't get hurt, wouldn't have conflict, or wouldn't ever have to move on from jobs or relationships or places.

I felt sick to my stomach about the way the situation was unfolding. There was no way to completely avoid conflict when I decided to walk away from my job. Thankfully, by the time I turned in my notice I had found a new position, but I still had to decide how to engage or avoid the conflict with my boss. I wondered if I should just lie and pretend that I was simply making a career move. I wondered if I actually had to tell my boss that some of his actions were unacceptable to me and that I no longer felt comfortable working under him.

I know which road I would have taken earlier in my life. I would have simply ducked out, omitted the hard truths, maybe even thrown in some niceties, and never looked back. Working downtown the year before had been an experience rife with conflict. I knew I was living into my calling, yet nothing about that year was easy. I lived in a house with nine other people who were full of emotions, expectations, and baggage. We had committed to living in intentional community, meaning that we were supposed to agree on every decision by consensus. Conflict was around every corner for us, especially when our jobs constantly drained us.

The tension in our house often centered on petty arguments: how many bananas we should buy and who wasn't doing their dishes. But it was also about what to do to help our housemate who was slipping back into alcoholism. The ongoing conflict was exhausting. It was like climbing up and down mountains every single day.

Wading through conflict again and again, however, made it easier for me to know when to hold back and when to engage. I became less tempted to slip into the assumption that a messy situation meant I wasn't in the right place. I became more confident in standing up for others or for my own values. I became more adept at recognizing the underlying expectations that fueled almost all the disagreements in our house. Being surrounded by conflict for almost an entire year wasn't pleasant, but it did build up muscles that would have been hard to get otherwise.

Higher-stakes conflicts met me in other places that year. The church where I worked, like so many churches, was mired in conflict. Much of it simmered just under the surface—nonexistent in the view of some of the leadership but immediate in the view of some of those stuck in the boiling waters. As a relative outsider, I found myself caught between the two. I mostly watched as battles unfolded around me. It was messy, and everyone suffered. People felt unheard, and long-running programs were closed. Relationships ended. Power was misused.

The church conflict was uncomfortable and unfortunate, but I knew my calling had led me to that position. I stuck it out for the entirety of my term there, and by staying, I learned a host of lessons. I climbed mountains and built muscles. And the next year, when I faced the uncomfortable situation with a boss who had been my friend, I had the muscles to pull myself up that mountain. I realized that conflict is sometimes necessary; we can all learn from it. Conflict doesn't mean we have somehow gotten off the path.

My boss and I sat down to talk after I turned in my two-week notice. It wasn't an easy conversation. I knew I needed to speak honestly with him, but I didn't want to sit across from him and say what I felt I should say. The situation was unpleasant, yet I had covered hills and mountains of conflict before, and my muscles were getting bigger. I made it through.

Conflict is not the only obstacle we will encounter on the path toward calling. We will become stronger in other areas as we encounter difficult situations and practice walking through them. As we walk into our calling, we will continue to encounter conflicts, along with fear, shame, insecurity, and loss—and all the situations that spin out of those difficulties and emotions.

But we practice. We climb hills; we climb mountains; we build up muscles. We become resilient.

To get up the mountains, we may have to give ourselves pep talks or ask our best friends and biggest supporters to help us. Occasionally, we might even have to climb the summit of our fears on all fours. We do it again and again, and when we climb up on our knees and still make it to the top and find God there, those times will become our rallying cry.

We follow our calling, and we practice being brave. We lean into our themes and practice being vulnerable. When our lives of calling take us to hard places, we practice holding the hands of the dying. We practice giving sermons even when our knees shake under our skirts. We practice showing up—showing up at our office jobs, showing up for coffee with struggling friends, showing up for our spouses with our full presence. We show up, and we let ourselves be seen. We practice forgiveness. We practice conflict. We practice letting go, and we practice loving others and ourselves.

We practice. We climb. We learn not to doubt our place and our calling when things get difficult. We walk west—even when it means that we are pulling ourselves upward with sticks or climbing on our knees.

Walking into our callings doesn't get easier. At least it hasn't for me, and it hasn't for any of the people I admire. We will continue to face curve balls—new bosses, new job descriptions, new family situations, and new conflict. Jobs, relationships, and lives will sometimes end unexpectedly. Some of our dreams will die, and so will some of our favorite people.

The terrain we walk does not get easier. The grace is that God, Emmanuel, travels with us, and we get stronger.

As we walk into the path of our callings, we will gain endurance to run the race that is marked out for us. We will struggle and be out of breath, but we will meet God on the way up and on the way down those hills and mountains. We will find that we handle conflict, fear, and long days better. We will be able to own our stories and own our place within them—even when struggles try to shake us loose from that firm foundation.

Chapter 10

Monte do Gozo– Seeing Your Dreams on the Horizon

I woke up with a smile on my face. I was on my way to Monte do Gozo! Monte do Gozo, or Mount of Joy, is the hill that sits right outside the city of Santiago. Traditionally, pilgrims have stopped at Monte do Gozo in order to see the tips of the Cathedral of Santiago in the distance. I was getting close to Santiago. Monte do Gozo was only a short day's hike away.

At least, it should have been a short day's hike.

I left the hostel with pep in my step. The bar down the road was the only place open, so I had breakfast there under the gaze of mounted animal heads. Locals argued about politics as I ate toast and apricot jam with *café con leche* for probably the thirtieth time that month. Fortified, I hit the trail.

The road from the town of O Pedrouzo, where I started my morning, to Monte do Gozo was supposed to be sixteen kilometers. There was a problem, though. It started when I stumbled upon Juanma and Maica, my retired Sevillian friends, earlier than I did most days.

After weeks of running into each other on the trails in the afternoon or in the hostels in the evening, we joyfully resigned ourselves to the fact that we couldn't seem to get rid of each other. They were wonderful company, and it was exciting to near the end of my journey with people who had been my companions for such a long distance. The three of us stopped for a leisurely coffee. We collected a stamp inside the café and then continued on together.

Then the problem arose. Maica and I were slowly walking along, chatting. She is short with a soft voice and a strong accent intensified by at least four decades of smoking. I was frequently bent over trying to hear her better, with her patiently trying to get me to understand. At some point, we became so involved in trying to communicate that we missed the yellow arrows and veered off the Camino.

It took us a while to figure out what had happened, but we began to notice that there were no other pilgrims around (and pilgrims had been buzzing past us all morning). Typically, Juanma walked ahead of us and at intervals waited for us to catch up. But we never caught up to him. Where was he?

We realized what had happened. So close to our final destination, we were lost.

Thankfully, our situation mostly struck us as funny—getting lost on our last real day hiking the Camino was fitting for the journey. We kept asking for directions, and people told us to continue going down the street we were on. We doubted whether the road would actually get us to Monte do Gozo, and we worried that Juanma was waiting for us somewhere else, but we continued on, chatting the whole way. Eventually, we made it to Monte do Gozo and spotted Juanma, sitting at a café near the entrance to the town, having a cold drink.

In Monte do Gozo, on top of the hill, is a monument built for the Pope's last visit to Santiago. Supposedly, from this monument it is possible to spot the spires of Santiago's cathedral in the distance. I had been waiting to see Santiago for over a month. I hiked westward each day, and I would finally be able to see the city and the characteristic three spires of the cathedral.

Before looking for the cathedral, I went to the hostel for a shower and one of my last rounds of washing my hiking clothes by hand. Then I made my way to the papal monument. I sat on the hill in the grass and scanned the horizon for the cathedral as I let my hair dry in the sun. I had no luck whatsoever.

I wasn't entirely disappointed that I couldn't spot my destination on the horizon. Arriving at Monte do Gozo, it felt strange to be so close to the end of my journey. I was close, but not there yet. I was sitting on that hill in the sunshine, drying my wet hair and feeling a strange tension.

These days, lots of pilgrims don't stop and stay the night in Monte do Gozo. They rush straight into Santiago. I had decided beforehand that I wanted to stop, but once I arrived in Monte do Gozo, once I knew that my final destination was only a handful of miles down the road, it was incredibly tempting to rush into town and storm Santiago's plaza.

Sitting on that hill, I felt a growing sense of restlessness, knowing that Santiago was within reach. Walking across an entire country on foot had been such a long journey that sometimes I forgot that I would eventually arrive. Sometimes I forgot that I even had a destination—that I wasn't just walking circles in the middle of the countryside for no reason at all. While I felt tremendous excitement to make it to Santiago, I also had feelings of fear and sadness. This life-changing journey was about to end.

Eventually, after my hair had dried and I had searched every inch of the horizon for the cathedral's spires, I walked back to the hostel. I made a pot of tea and met some new friends. In a total surprise, I also ran into my Korean friends, who had walked ahead of me a few days before. I caught up with Juanma and Maica later that evening, too. As we all sat around the table, Juanma noted that the place to see Santiago's cathedral wasn't the papal monument. There was a pilgrim monument on the other side of the hill. From *that* monument, you could see the cathedral.

In a race against sunset, I got up from the table and quickly hiked through a field in the direction of the pilgrim monument, which was made of two giant, bronze pilgrim statues, dressed in medieval garb, tipping their hats toward the city. Right before the statues came into view, I glanced to my right and saw it. The cathedral of Santiago! I screamed with surprise and joy. Tiny on the horizon, the cathedral poked its three spires into a pink sky.

I joined the pilgrim statues tipping their hats to Santiago in the distance by symbolically tipping my sunglasses in the same manner toward the cathedral. I sat on their big bronze feet and soaked up my final sunset on the trail with a view of the cathedral. I felt immensely thankful and excited to sit so close to Santiago.

That night, I stayed in Monte do Gozo to force myself to stop. I wanted the time to process my adventure, my feelings, and my journey. Sitting at the monument, I took the chance to think back over the beautiful places and the quirky and openhearted people I had met over the last thirty-one days and hundreds of miles. I took in the blisters, bruises, and bandages. I looked inside and wondered if I had sorted myself out. I wondered how I had miraculously made it within view of my destination after all.

Years later, in my apartment in Denver, I was taken back to the moment of catching the Santiago cathedral in the distance. I stopped and grabbed the sides of the kitchen sink, my hands soapy and the pot only half washed. A wave of emotions rolled over me. How have I made it to this place after all?

I had been on the journey of my calling for so long that I forgot I was actually on a trajectory meant to go somewhere. While walking painful step after painful step and taking in beauty in each mountain peak, it's hard to imagine that I could possibly forget I was on a journey, that I was actually getting somewhere. But that's exactly what happened.

Ever since I was a little girl, I have thought that my calling would lead me to the mission field. I have been able to realize along this journey that my calling is not about a destination or a career path. My calling is the theme of walking alongside people, of journeying with them.

I had to let go of my expectations of how my calling and my dreams would play out. Expectations are some of life's most potent and subtlest manifestations of our dreams. I finally got to a point where I could recognize my expectations for what they were and realize how deeply they ran in both my subconscious and in my actions.

I finally came to a place of reckoning and a place of healing. I would walk west. I would sort through my baggage. I would walk in faith, following the ways the arrows of the Spirit led me. I would accompany and journey with whomever was in my path. That meant

I was living into my calling when I worked hard jobs with people experiencing homelessness, even when those positions almost bankrupted my ability to remember that goodness wins in the end. Understanding my calling in this way also meant I was living into my calling when I worked as an office manager for a season, holding together all the loose ends of a start-up company. It meant that everything from managing phone calls and office supplies to creating marketing plans and writing press releases was just as much a part of my calling as serving the homeless in the downtown area.

Later, I transitioned into a job in which I worked with Catholic nuns, helping to direct their spiritual retreat center. It was good work that allowed me to journey with people, even if it was a bit understimulating. I haven't always been happy with my career path, but I have come to a place of understanding my calling that settles the restlessness within me. I invested in that job, but I also spent time mentoring young women. I found a homeless shelter where I could volunteer. I continued to walk westward.

All the while, my husband, David, and I continued to talk and dream about missions. Before we started dating, we both individually thought our callings would take us to overseas ministry. Once our relationship grew serious and we decided to marry, we dreamed of doing international ministry together. We talked about missions, and every once in a while I even allowed myself to dream about it happening.

When David graduated from seminary, we began talking with different mission-sending agencies. The conversations left me with a mix of excitement for what could be and fear of what might never be. I was afraid that we would never find a place where we would both be able to serve in ways that fit our individual callings. Sometimes, as we explored options, that fear seemed reasonable.

Despite my fears, we were offered an overseas ministry position. We were asked to become field personnel, or missionaries, in Phnom Penh, Cambodia. The position was ours for the taking.

Sorting out and walking into our callings are hard enough on our own. Sometimes they are doubly difficult to do with someone else. I know how easy it is to miss arrows, even when your destination is so close. Walking with someone else at your side can make things easier, and it can make things harder. Most often, it seems to be a mix of both.

We prayed. We talked to everyone we thought might have a shred of wisdom or insight for us. We hoped God would send us a text message.

All through the journey, we said that we were open to living and serving any place in the world, as long as the work would allow us both to live out our callings. Cambodia was nowhere on our radar, but an opportunity to live and work there was presented to us. My husband would have the opportunity to equip local pastors and church planters in need of training. I would have the opportunity to use economic development projects to journey with some of Cambodia's poorest people.

We were intrigued, but we weren't sure. In the end, we didn't get a text message from God. Instead, we had a conversation that lasted late into the night. We couldn't deny that these two positions were good fits for each of our callings. We said yes.

I'll admit that I didn't immediately have the strength to look into the horizon, to see if I could spot the dream that I had been walking toward for such a long, long time. It was not until the next day, standing in our kitchen, bent over the soapy sink, that I looked up. With the decision made and the apartment empty, I stood at the sink in my pajamas and finally, halfway through washing the dishes, let myself look to the horizon.

I stopped. I let myself breathe, and I allowed myself to look at the decision we had made and the future we had accepted. I wasn't sure that I would see my dream on the horizon. I was afraid I'd see nothing but urban sprawl, no cathedral in the distance. Yet I let myself look. I let myself feel and imagine, and I felt like I did in the middle of that field in Monte do Gozo. I spotted the spires of my Santiago. I let myself look and feel the pangs of excitement and the tension of seeing my dream on the horizon after all this time, after all those painful steps.

I stood at the sink and cried big, heavy tears.

I was afraid of looking into the near future and seeing a mistake. I was afraid that when I looked ahead, I wouldn't see anything there after all. I was also afraid that when I looked ahead, I would see precisely what I had been journeying toward.

It's terrifying to take hold of the thing we have always thought we wanted. Leaning into our dreams and walking into a manifestation of our calling is scary. When we actually get a chance to take hold of it, there is always the option that we will fail—and the possibility of failure feels incredibly heavy when we are talking about our dreams. When faced with the opportunity to take hold of my dreams, I now find myself wondering about all the "what ifs." What if I'm not good at it? What if I made the wrong decision? What if the journey I am on ends and the next one is completely different? What if I have to start again from scratch?

I have felt the sensation of fear enough times to be able to name it for what it is. Sometimes fear tells us something is wrong, but more often than not, fear tells us merely that we are afraid. We are fragile. We are at the cusp of big risks, and we are vulnerable. Usually, we need to walk in faith with our Creator, follow our calling, and take the leap.

Standing there at the sink, I also felt the tension that comes when we near a goal after a long journey. It's a feeling similar to the emotions I felt before a graduation ceremony, before a big move, or before my wedding. There is a sense that things are changing in a dramatic and good way, but it's still a bit unnerving.

Standing in the kitchen, I also felt a rush of relief and affirmation. All these steps had added up after all. There was a destination. The horizon held an image of my future that seemed foreign and challenging, but it also looked like the image my calling had led me toward all this time.

No matter how much time we have to prepare for it, it's scary to take hold of the things we have dreamed about and worked toward. Finding our dreams within our reach makes us feel surprisingly vulnerable. Taking hold of them seems risky.

Seeing our dreams close at hand makes us revisit our fears and our expectations. We can live in those fears, or we can think about all the beautiful and testing moments that have led us to that very point. We can be afraid and wander more years in the desert, or we can tip our hats with joy to the next destination of our callings.

Chapter 11

Santiago–Celebrations and New Destinations

I was like a kid on Christmas. I couldn't sleep. Normally, I was one of the last people out of the pilgrim hostels in the morning. I liked to wait until there was enough light coming into the dorms so that I didn't have to get ready in the dark or try to pack quietly as others slept. Not so on my last day. I was only five kilometers away from Santiago, and I was wide awake.

Outside the hostel, I met up with my friends from Seville, who were usually early risers, and we decided to walk into Santiago together. Juanma and Maica were two of my favorite people on the Camino, and it was a pleasure to walk into the city with them on our final day.

We walked the five kilometers into the city, stopping for a coffee along the way. There was something about being so close to Santiago that made me want to slow down and take it all in as observantly as possible, even if another part of me wanted to run straight into the city.

We finally made it into the center of Santiago. Juanma, our fearless navigator, looked at the map while Maica and I chatted away (we didn't let him out of sight this time). The city began to transform from a modern urban metropolis into a stone- and moss-covered medieval capital. We could sense that we were making our way into the historic heart of Santiago.

We wound through stone streets and past beautiful churches and buildings. I knew we were getting close to the cathedral, but I couldn't place exactly where we were in the city. We passed Santiago's old seminary and then walked through a stone arch. As I walked through the arch, I realized exactly where we were—we were walking right into the plaza of the cathedral in Santiago de Compostela.

We took the plaza by storm, banging our walking sticks, blowing whistles, and hugging in celebration. It was a feeling like no other, a mix of triumph, joy, relief, and even a bit of the apprehension that comes at the end of a journey. We hugged each other. We hugged the ground. After walking toward this destination for almost five hundred miles and finally arriving, we experienced a huge sense of accomplishment, happiness, and celebration.

After three dozen pictures, a stroll around the plaza, and a dance with the Galician bagpipe player serenading us, we went back around the cathedral to find the pilgrims' office so that we could get our *compostelas*. We got there right as they opened. I was so excited about receiving my *compostela* that I made the guy filling out my certificate laugh.

Compostelas are official documents from the Catholic Church, still issued in the original Latin, that authenticate pilgrimages to Santiago. The officials examined our pilgrim credentials and stamps to make sure we hadn't skipped any portions of the Camino, especially within the last one hundred kilometers. Then they translated our first names into Latin-sounding first names, filled in our *compostelas,* and gave them the official stamp of the cathedral. *Lorena Brewer* had officially completed her pilgrimage!

Feeling properly authenticated, we settled in for a celebratory breakfast of *chocolate y churros.* I had started my Camino in Pamplona with *churros,* so fried dough dipped in chocolate seemed the perfect way to finish it.

We headed back to the cathedral to look around inside and to get seats for the daily pilgrim Mass. Before long, there was standing room only. While Juanma saved our seats, I walked around the cathedral and looked through the crowd. I spotted a few friends I had made along the way.

By this point, I had attended countless Spanish Masses, but this one was a pilgrim Mass in the Cathedral of *Santiago*. This Mass was special. It had been our destination all along. The Mass began with a tiny nun attempting to teach us the hymns that were to be sung later.

We sang our hymns, and then the priest read the verses from the Gospel of John in which Jesus said, "*I am the bread of life.*" After eating so much bread along the way, and experiencing its energy-giving power, the passage was fitting.

Then, addressing the pilgrims who had arrived and registered with the church office that day, the priest called out all the places where each of us had started our pilgrimages and where we were from. I was excited to hear him call out "*one pilgrim from the USA who started in Pamplona.*" A couple of friends further into the cathedral turned around to give me a thumbs-up.

Next was the *botafumeiro*, Santiago's famous incense burner. According to legend, the *botafumeiro* was necessary because the pilgrims smelled so badly by the end of their journey that the church needed pounds of incense to cover the odor. The *botafumeiro* weighs around 175 pounds, is over 5 feet tall, and is filled with about 88 pounds of charcoal and incense. It's made of ornate silver and looks far too precious to actually be in use—especially to be swung around the cathedral's ceiling by a rope.

Eight priests help pull and swing the *botafumeiro*. Before long, the incense burner started to *fly* through the cathedral. Some people have estimated that it moves along at speeds of over forty miles per hour. It went right over our heads, so close that I ducked every time, and then it swung upwards until it almost touched the ceiling. By the time it reached full speed, the incense burner was consumed in a ball of fire, spreading a cloud of incense all over the cathedral.

We smelled it. We tasted it. We breathed it in.

After the Mass, we took in all the pilgrim rituals the city had to offer. We made our way through the cathedral's crypt to see the box that supposedly holds the bones of St. James the Apostle, or *Santiago* in Spanish. We then walked back upstairs in the cathedral and "hugged" the statue of St. James in the altar of the cathedral and whispered a prayer in his ear.

As the afternoon came to a close, I parted with friends for a bit to walk and think. Then, as I did almost every other day of the Camino, I spent the last part of my day sitting in the plaza, soaking up the last rays of sunlight, and reflecting back on the way I had come.

As I write this, I'm surprised to find myself in a Santiago of sorts. While I am not yet in Cambodia, I'm finally headed back overseas, this time as a missionary. In the process of actually saying *yes* to this position, I realized how scary it had been to dream about living into this manifestation of my calling. When those dreams, the ones we couldn't even say out loud for fear that they would crumble on us, do appear on the horizon, when we walk through their plazas, when we breathe in the incense of their reality, our feelings of excitement, joy, and celebration are all the greater.

Pilgrimages are hard. Pilgrimages on foot and pilgrimages into our callings require a lot of energy. Sometimes they require all that we have inside us. So, when we reach a milestone, it is important to celebrate. The milestone might be that we have walked a hundred kilometers or that we have finally escaped the meseta, or it might be that we preached our first sermon—in a seminary class or to a real-life congregation—or that we are halfway through our degree program. Maybe we were finally offered an overseas missionary assignment, or maybe we talked to our first client, and even if it didn't feel completely comfortable, we didn't blow it. Let's celebrate our accomplishments, even the small ones. Those small milestones mean that we are on the move.

I love to celebrate, and I love to do it with other people. I know that I need people to struggle alongside me and to guide me on my journey, but I also need people to celebrate with me. We are told to rejoice with those who rejoice, and sometimes that commandment is harder than weeping with those who weep. Celebrating with others, especially when we aren't able to identify anything to celebrate in our own journeys, can cause us to wrestle all over again with the vulnerable possibility that our own milestones may or may not happen. Celebrating with others can bring us face to face with our fears and our hopes, but it can also tie us to our communities.

Celebrating also ties us to our stories. Walking through the rituals of pilgrimage in Santiago—the tastes, the smells, the hugs, and the pictures—means that even now, years later, I can remember what it felt like to stand in that plaza with a deep feeling of joy and gratitude for the journey, for the people I met along the way, and for the faithfulness of my God. When we hug statues in a cathedral, when we don black gowns and funny hats or expensive white dresses, we step out of the ordinary and create markers for us to hold on to.

We mark the moments that mark us so that we can remember who we are and the journey we have traveled. It's why the Old Testament is full of altar building and mandated celebrations. It's why I believe in dinners on the patio with red wine and day trips to the tops of nearby mountains. It's why I value my community and my friends who surround me to squeal or cry or say, "Cambodia—that sounds perfect!"

The morning after our arrival in Santiago, we woke, ate breakfast, and then looked around at all the other beautiful churches, monasteries, and old buildings in the city. I spent the rest of my time just taking in the accomplishment with good friends.

I arrived in Santiago about a week before my flight out of Spain. Even though I had planned to stay there for a couple of days to see the city, catch up with other pilgrims, and relish in the accomplishment, I had some days to spare.

One of the many beautiful things of the Camino de Santiago is that for the duration of your walk to Santiago, you don't have to make many daily decisions. You wake up. You walk. When you get tired, you look for a pilgrims' hostel and stop. For an indecisive person like me, not having to make decisions was wonderful.

After over a month of waking up each day and walking west, my arrival in Santiago meant it was time to start making decisions again. I had flirted with the idea of walking to Finisterre for most of my Camino, or at least after it started to look like I would arrive in Santiago well before my flight date.

The Camino to Finisterre is almost a coda to the Camino to Santiago. Traditionally, pilgrims have walked the extra distance from the city of Santiago to Finisterre on the western coast of Spain. Finisterre, which means "end of the world" in Latin, was thought to be the westernmost point of Europe and therefore the westernmost part of the known world. Pilgrims walked to the rocky coast and watched the sun set into the sea before turning around and walking home.

During the last week or so of walking that led up to Santiago, I started to change my mind. Although it's *only* an eighty-nine-kilometer walk from Santiago to Finisterre, I could feel myself winding down. My last big walking day ended with pain in both ankles and two new blisters. Maybe Santiago should be my pilgrimage's final destination.

I thought that maybe I would take a bus from Santiago and spend my extra days in a guesthouse on the coast somewhere. I toyed with the idea of heading down to Portugal for a few days. I wasn't sure what I wanted to do.

On my last morning in Santiago, I packed up my backpack in the hostel like usual. I picked up my boots and noticed that, although I'd mostly stopped wearing them, they still showed the wear of hundreds of miles of hiking. I decided not to carry them around with me anymore. I didn't foresee my future time on my sabbatical requiring hiking boots. I zipped up my backpack without them and tossed them in the wastebasket on my way out of the hostel.

I left the hostel to meet Juanma and Maica for breakfast before they boarded a bus back to Seville. They were headed home, but I still wasn't sure where I was headed next.

After breakfast and a tearful goodbye, I realized I wasn't ready to stop. I wanted to keep going. I walked back to the hostel alone and pulled my boots out of the trash can. I decided to walk to Finisterre after all.

There's something about arriving at a destination that makes me want to stay. I want to set up camp there. I want to unpack my boxes and put some things on the wall. I want to settle in. I'd like the work of getting there to be over, at least for a good while.

I want something solid to plan around.

I think it would be wonderfully refreshing to arrive, to celebrate, and then to enjoy living that good life forever. Now that my calling is taking me to journey with people overseas in Cambodia, I'd like to think that I will never have to struggle again with where my calling is taking me. It would be nice if I could stay put and never have to look around for those arrows or find myself at another dead-end path at the top of a mountain. I'd like to arrive and let the hard days of following my calling be lessons in the past.

The truth looks a lot more like the story my pilgrim friend, Denise, shared over tea at a little pilgrim hostel high in the mountains. Denise and her husband, Mark, are from Tasmania and were walking the Camino together for the second time. They were walking slowly, looking around every church, monastery, or café that interested them.

I ran into them several times throughout the later portion of my Camino, but it was the day I sat with them outside our hostel in Rabanal del Camino that stands out in my memory. Several of us had gathered around a table in the late afternoon and were warming our hands with cups of tea when Denise shared a story that I'm still processing.

Denise told us that on her previous Camino she met a monk in one of the monasteries along the way. The monk told Denise, as she was reflecting on her pilgrimage, that when a pilgrim walks west for so long, something special happens. West is where the sun dies. As pilgrims walk west, day after day, something in them dies too, he said. In the space of that death, something new will be born.

Denise wasn't so sure, and I was a bit skeptical as I heard her tell the story. Remarkably, though, Denise said that the wisdom the monk shared was true for her. She said it didn't happen immediately. Or at least she didn't realize the change inside her immediately. Only after she returned home did she find the space for something new to be born within her.

I meditated on that story long after I stopped passing Mark and Denise on the trail. I kept looking inside myself for a possible death or for some sign of new growth.

The Camino was like a long, painful massage. It hurt, but the reality was that those knots in me needed to be untangled. I needed to walk west, where the sun dies, and let some things go inside of me too. I needed to learn how to relax, take breaks, and be present to the people around me. I needed to learn how to look for and follow God's path. I needed to dig through my baggage and lighten my load. I needed to learn how to stop trying to *make it work*. I needed to remember why I was walking the path of my calling in the first place.

After a couple of days in Santiago, I discovered that my need to control my destination had lessened. I realized Denise's monk was right. In that open space, something new was born inside of me. I was able to lift my backpack back onto my shoulders and continue my journey to a new destination.

Following our callings is much the same. All I wanted for so long was to arrive. I wanted to arrive at a missionary assignment until that felt too far out of reach. After that, I simply wanted to arrive somewhere solid. I wanted to be able to stop chasing my calling from town to town. I wanted to stop having conversations with my reflection, asking myself what I wanted or how I was going to make this new thing, this new problem, this new twist work.

Cambodia feels like an arrival of sorts for me. It feels like the end of a long journey. If I'm not careful, I can let myself think that this destination is what my calling, my whole journey, was about. Yet Cambodia alone is not my calling or my final destination.

Cambodia is simply the next stage of my journey. It's where the arrows are leading me, leading us. It's a dream on the horizon, and I'm thankful for this stage of the journey—so thankful that we are constantly finding new ways to celebrate it.

I have walked a lot of miles to get here. Those miles have included long, lonely stretches through stormy flatlands and steep inclines. The miles have been full of sharing stories and sharing plates full of *churros* with friends, coworkers, and fellow pilgrims. I've had ugly-faced cries and squeals of joy.

I've carried around baggage, and I've let some go. I've changed footgear, and I've changed the way I look at the world and my place in it. I've seen some of my dreams come true, and I've hit some dead ends. These lessons and these experiences have all changed me. Following my calling has shaped me and made me grateful, and my calling has left me with scars and limps. It's been the hardest and richest thing I've ever done.

Even now, when a piece of me would like to arrive at a destination and stay there, I know that this is not what calling is about. Calling is not a job. It's not a title. It's not a destination. Calling is a journey, a pilgrimage. Calling is leading me now to a destination, but it compels me to keep watching for arrows, keep watching for rebirth, and keep watching for new destinations.

Calling. It's a pilgrimage. The metaphor reminds us to relax and look for the Holy Spirit's direction as we go. It helps us reframe struggles and dissatisfaction, and it gives us perspective—for the good days and the bad. Understanding the metaphor of calling as pilgrimage also helps us understand that our whole lives are a journey of ministry.

These journeys of ministry, these callings of ours, are beautiful pilgrimages that take us to surprising places and transform us at each stage. They allow us to walk with God and to walk with others. The path is full of blisters and beautiful cathedrals. It's a journey of five hundred miles and more, but it's a path I am grateful to be walking.

Acknowledgments

To my fellow travelers, both named and unnamed, on the Camino and in my regular life, thank you.

Thanks especially to my husband, David, who is the best traveling companion, editor, and friend a person could ask for. Thanks also to Jennay, Annie, Alyssa, and the many other friends who have read and helped shaped this book, and to the fellow pilgrims, especially Krystal and Amanda, who have helped me spot arrows when I was lost and walked some of the long, lonely stretches of calling alongside me. Jamie, Essam, and Caley, thank you for your unwavering encouragement.

I am so grateful to Pam Durso and Meredith Stone for realizing the need for this book and for encouraging me to write it.

Mom, Dad, and family, thank you for helping me get on the path and for supporting me as it continues to take me to unexpected places.

Ultimately, I give thanks to the God who continues to call me, and all of us, onward.

Other available titles from

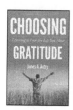

Contextualizing the Gospel
A Homiletic Commentary on 1 Corinthians
Brian L. Harbour

Harbour examines every part of Paul's letter, providing a rich resource for those who want to struggle with the difficult texts as well as the simple texts, who want to know how God's word—all of it—intersects with their lives today. *978-1-57312-589-5 240 pages/pb* **$19.00**

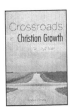

Crossroads in Christian Growth
W. Loyd Allen

Authentic Christian life presents spiritual crises and we struggle to find a hero walking with God at a crossroads. With wisdom and sincerity, W. Loyd Allen presents Jesus as our example and these crises as stages in the journey of growth we each take toward maturity in Christ. *978-1-57312-753-0 164 pages/pb* **$15.00**

A Divine Duet
Ministry and Motherhood
Alicia Davis Porterfield, ed.

Each essay in this inspiring collection is as different as the mother-minister who wrote it, from theologians to chaplains, inner-city ministers to rural-poverty ministers, youth pastors to preachers, mothers who have adopted, birthed, and done both. *978-1-57312-676-2 146 pages/pb* **$16.00**

Ethics as if Jesus Mattered
Essays in Honor of Glen H. Stassen
Rick Axtell, Michelle Tooley, Michael L. Westmoreland-White, eds.

Ethics as if Jesus Mattered will introduce Stassen's work to a new generation, advance dialogue and debate in Christian ethics, and inspire more faithful discipleship just as it honors one whom the contributors consider a mentor. *978-1-57312-695-3 234 pages/pb* **$18.00**

Ezekiel (Smyth & Helwys Annual Bible Study series)
God's Presence in Performance
William D. Shiell

Through a four-session Bible study for individuals and groups, Shiell interprets the book of Ezekiel as a four-act drama to be told to adult, children, and youth groups living out their faith in a strange, new place. The book encourages congregations to listen to God's call, accept where God has planted them, surrender the shame of their past, receive a new heart from God, and allow God to breathe new life into them.

Teaching Guide 978-1-57312-755-4 192 pages/pb **$14.00**

Study Guide 978-1-57312-756-1 126 pages/pb **$6.00**

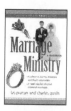

Marriage Ministry: A Guidebook
Bo Prosser and Charles Qualls

This book is equally helpful for ministers, for nearly/newlywed couples, and for thousands of couples across our land looking for fresh air in their marriages. *1-57312-432-X 160 pages/pb* **$16.00**

A Hungry Soul Desperate to Taste God's Grace
Honest Prayers for Life

Charles Qualls

Part of how we *see* God is determined by how we *listen* to God. There is so much noise and movement in the world that competes with images of God. This noise would drown out God's beckoning voice and distract us. Charles Qualls's newest book offers readers prayers for that journey toward the meaning and mystery of God. *978-1-57312-648-9 152 pages/pb* **$14.00**

If Jesus Isn't the Answer . . . He Sure Asks the Right Questions!
J. Daniel Day

Taking eleven of Jesus' questions as its core, Day invites readers into their own conversation with Jesus. Equal parts testimony, theological instruction, pastoral counseling, and autobiography, the book is ultimately an invitation to honest Christian discipleship.

978-1-57312-797-4 148 pages/pb **$16.00**

I'm Trying to Lead . . . Is Anybody Following?
The Challenge of Congregational Leadership in the Postmodern World

Charles B. Bugg

Bugg provides us with a view of leadership that has theological integrity, honors the diversity of church members, and reinforces the brave hearts of church leaders who offer vision and take risks in the service of Christ and the church. *978-1-57312-731-8 136 pages/pb* **$13.00**

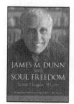

James M. Dunn and Soul Freedom
Aaron Douglas Weaver

James Milton Dunn, over the last fifty years, has been the most aggressive Baptist proponent for religious liberty in the United States. Soul freedom—voluntary, uncoerced faith and an unfettered individual conscience before God—is the basis of his understanding of church-state separation and the historic Baptist basis of religious liberty. *978-1-57312-590-1 224 pages/pb* **$18.00**

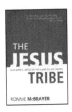

The Jesus Tribe
Following Christ in the Land of the Empire
Ronnie McBrayer

The Jesus Tribe fleshes out the implications, possibilities, contradictions, and complexities of what it means to live within the Jesus Tribe and in the shadow of the American Empire.

978-1-57312-592-5 208 pages/pb **$17.00**

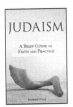

Judaism
A Brief Guide to Faith and Practice
Sharon Pace

Sharon Pace's newest book is a sensitive and comprehensive introduction to Judaism. What is it like to be born into the Jewish community? How does belief in the One God and a universal morality shape the way in which Jews see the world? How does one find meaning in life and the courage to endure suffering? How does one mark joy and forge community ties?

978-1-57312-644-1 144 pages/pb **$16.00**

Living Call
An Old Church and a Young Minister Find Life Together
Tony Lankford

This light look at church and ministry highlights the dire need for fidelity to the vocation of church leadership. It also illustrates Lankford's conviction that the historic, local congregation has a beautiful, vibrant, and hopeful future.

978-1-57312-702-8 112 pages/pb **$12.00**

Looking Around for God
The Strangely Reverent Observations of an Unconventional Christian
James A. Autry

Looking Around for God, Autry's tenth book, is in many ways his most personal. In it he considers his unique life of faith and belief in God. Autry is a former Fortune 500 executive, author, poet, and consultant whose work has had a significant influence on leadership thinking.

978-157312-484-3 144 pages/pb **$16.00**

Meeting Jesus Today
For the Cautious, the Curious, and the Committed
Jeanie Miley

Meeting Jesus Today, ideal for both individual study and small groups, is intended to be used as a workbook. It is designed to move readers from studying the Scriptures and ideas within the chapters to recording their journey with the Living Christ.

978-1-57312-677-9 320 pages/pb **$19.00**

The Ministry Life
101 Tips for Ministers' Spouses
John and Anne Killinger

While no pastor does his or her work alone, roles for a spouse or partner are much more flexible and fluid in the twenty-first century than they once were. Spouses who want to support their minister-mates' vocation may wonder where to begin. The Killingers' suggestions are notable for their range of interests; whatever your talents may be, the Killingers have identified a way to put those gifts to work in tasks both large and small.

978-1-57312-769-1 252 pages/pb **$19.00**

The Ministry Life
101 Tips for New Ministers
John Killinger

Sharing years of wisdom from more than fifty years in ministry and teaching, *The Ministry Life: 101 Tips for New Ministers* by John Killinger is filled with practical advice and wisdom for a minister's day-to-day tasks as well as advice on intellectual and spiritual habits to keep ministers of any age healthy and fulfilled. *978-1-57312-662-5 244 pages/pb* **$19.00**

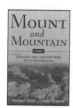

Mount and Mountain
Vol. 1: A Reverend and a Rabbi Talk About the Ten Commandments
Rami Shapiro and Michael Smith

Mount and Mountain represents the first half of an interfaith dialogue—a dialogue that neither preaches nor placates but challenges its participants to work both singly and together in the task of reinterpreting sacred texts. Mike and Rami discuss the nature of divinity, the power of faith, the beauty of myth and story, the necessity of doubt, the achievements, failings, and future of religion, and, above all, the struggle to live ethically and in harmony with the way of God. *978-1-57312-612-0 144 pages/pb* **$15.00**

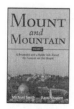

Mount and Mountain
Vol. 2: A Reverend and a Rabbi Talk About the Sermon on the Mount
Rami Shapiro and Michael Smith

This book, focused on the Sermon on the Mount, represents the second half of Mike and Rami's dialogue. In it, Mike and Rami explore the text of Jesus' sermon cooperatively, contributing perspectives drawn from their lives and religious traditions and seeking moments of illumination. *978-1-57312-654-0 254 pages/pb* **$19.00**

Of Mice and Ministers
Musings and Conversations About Life, Death, Grace, and Everything

Bert Montgomery

With stories about pains, joys, and everyday life, *Of Mice and Ministers* finds Jesus in some unlikely places and challenges us to do the same. From tattooed women ministers to saying the "N"-word to the brotherly kiss, Bert Montgomery takes seriously the lesson from Psalm 139—where can one go that God is not already there?   *978-1-57312-733-2 154 pages/pb* **$14.00**

Overcoming Adolescence
Growing Beyond Childhood into Maturity

Marion D. Aldridge

In *Overcoming Adolescence*, Marion D. Aldridge poses questions for adults of all ages to consider. His challenge to readers is one he has personally worked to confront: to grow up *all the way*—mentally, physically, academically, socially, emotionally, and spiritually. The key involves not only knowing how to work through the process but also how to recognize what may be contributing to our perpetual adolescence.

978-1-57312-577-2 156 pages/pb **$17.00**

Preacher Breath
Sermon & Essays

Kyndall Rae Rothaus

"The task of preaching is such an oddly wonderful, strangely beautiful experience. . . . Kyndall Rothaus's *Preacher Breath* is a worthy guide, leading the reader room by room with wisdom, depth, and a spiritual maturity far beyond her years, so that the preaching house becomes a holy, joyful home. . . . This book is soul kindle for a preacher's heart."

—Danielle Shroyer
Pastor and Author of *The Boundary-Breaking God*

978-1-57312-734-9 208 pages/pb **$16.00**

Quiet Faith
An Introvert's Guide to Spiritual Survival

Judson Edwards

In eight finely crafted chapters, Edwards looks at key issues like evangelism, interpreting the Bible, dealing with doubt, and surviving the church from the perspective of a confirmed, but sometimes reluctant, introvert. In the process, he offers some provocative insights that introverts will find helpful and reassuring.   *978-1-57312-681-6 144 pages/pb* **$15.00**

Reading Deuteronomy
(Reading the Old Testament series)
A Literary and Theological Commentary

Stephen L. Cook

A lost treasure for large segments of the modern world, the book of Deuteronomy powerfully repays contemporary readers' attention. God's presence and Word in Deuteronomy stir deep longing for God and move readers to a place of intimacy with divine otherness, holism, and will for person-centered community. The consistently theological interpretation reveals the centrality of Deuteronomy for faith and counters critical accusations about violence, intolerance, and polytheism in the book.   *978-1-57312-757-8 286 pages/pb* **$22.00**

Reading Hosea–Micah
(Reading the Old Testament series)
A Literary and Theological Commentary

Terence E. Fretheim

Terence E. Fretheim explores themes of indictment, judgment, and salvation in Hosea–Micah. The indictment against the people of God especially involves issues of idolatry, as well as abuse of the poor and needy. The effects of such behaviors are often horrendous in their severity. While God is often the subject of such judgments, the consequences, like fruit, grow out of the deed itself.   *978-1-57312-687-8 224 pages/pb* **$22.00**

Reflective Faith
A Theological Toolbox for Women

Tony W. Cartledge

In *Reflective Faith*, Susan Shaw offers a set of tools to explore difficult issues of biblical interpretation, theology, church history, and ethics—especially as they relate to women. Reflective faith invites intellectual struggle and embraces the unknown; it is a way of discipleship, a way to love God with your mind, as well as your heart, your soul, and your strength.

978-1-57312-719-6 292 pages/pb **$24.00**

Workbook 978-1-57312-754-7 164 pages/pb **$12.00**

Sessions with Psalms (Session Bible Studies series)
Prayers for All Seasons

Eric and Alicia D. Porterfield

Sessions with Psalms is a ten-session study unit designed to explore what it looks like for the words of the psalms to become the words of our prayers. Each session is followed by a thought-provoking page of questions that allow for a deeper experience of the scriptural passages. These resource pages can be used by seminar leaders during preparation and group discussion, as well as in individual Bible study.   *978-1-57312-768-4 136 pages/pb* **$14.00**

Sessions with Revelation (Session Bible Studies series)
The Final Days of Evil
David Sapp

David Sapp's careful guide through Revelation demonstrates that it is a letter of hope for believers; it is less about the last days of history than it is about the last days of evil. Without eliminating its mystery, Sapp unlocks Revelation's central truths so that its relevance becomes clear.
978-1-57312-706-6 166 pages/pb **$14.00**

Spacious
Exploring Faith and Place
Holly Sprink

Exploring where we are and why that matters to God is an ongoing process. If we are present and attentive, God creatively and continuously widens our view of the world. 978-1-57312-649-6 156 pages/pb **$16.00**

The Teaching Church
Congregation as Mentor
Christopher M. Hamlin / Sarah Jackson Shelton

Collected in *The Teaching Church: Congregation as Mentor* are the stories of the pastors who shared how congregations have shaped, nurtured, and, sometimes, broken their resolve to be faithful servants of God.
978-1-57312-682-3 112 pages/pb **$13.00**

Time for Supper
Invitations to Christ's Table
Brett Younger

Some scholars suggest that every meal in literature is a communion scene. Could every meal in the Bible be a communion text? Could every passage be an invitation to God's grace? At the Lord's Table we experience sorrow, hope, friendship, and forgiveness. These meditations on the Lord's Supper help us listen to the myriad of ways God invites us to gratefully, reverently, and joyfully share the cup of Christ.
978-1-57312-720-2 246 pages/pb **$18.00**

A Time to Laugh
Humor in the Bible

Mark E. Biddle

An extension of his well-loved seminary course on humor in the Bible, *A Time to Laugh* draws on Mark E. Biddle's command of Hebrew language and cultural subtleties to explore the ways humor was intentionally incorporated into Scripture. With characteristic liveliness, Biddle guides the reader through the stories of six biblical characters who did rather unexpected things. 978-1-57312-683-0 *164 pages/pb* **$14.00**

The World Is Waiting for You
Celebrating the 50th Ordination Anniversary of Addie Davis

Pamela R. Durso & LeAnn Gunter Johns, eds.

Hope for the church and the world is alive and well in the words of these gifted women. Keen insight, delightful observations, profound courage, and a gift for communicating the good news are woven throughout these sermons. The Spirit so evident in Addie's calling clearly continues in her legacy. 978-1-57312-732-5 *224 pages/pb* **$18.00**

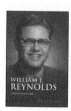

William J. Reynolds
Church Musician

David W. Music

William J. Reynolds is renowned among Baptist musicians, music ministers, song leaders, and hymnody students. In eminently readable style, David W. Music's comprehensive biography describes Reynolds's family and educational background, his career as a minister of music, denominational leader, and seminary professor. 978-1-57312-690-8 *358 pages/pb* **$23.00**

With Us in the Wilderness
Finding God's Story in Our Lives

Laura A. Barclay

What stories compose your spiritual biography? In *With Us in the Wilderness*, Laura Barclay shares her own stories of the intersection of the divine and the everyday, guiding readers toward identifying and embracing God's presence in their own narratives.

978-1-57312-721-9 *120 pages/pb* **$13.00**

Made in the USA
Charleston, SC
26 May 2015